TAKING THE KINGDOM

TAKING THE KINGDOM

But the saints of the most High shall take the kingdom,and possess the kingdom for ever, even for ever and ever.

Daniel 7:18

Elton F. Chesser

Taking The Kingdom

Elton F. Chesser

Scripture quotations are from the King James Version of the Bible.

Printed in the United States of America

ISBN: 978-1-961482-02-9

Dedicated to the memory of Warren D. Hilderbrand, my pastor from my elementary school age years until I left home for college. It was his amazing teaching skills which inspired me to study and aspire to be the kind of Bible teacher he was.

Contents

Preface
Foreword
Chapter 1. The Genesis of Evil
Chapter 2. The Spirit World and Calvary
Chapter 3. The Birth of the Church Age
Chapter 4. God's Timing
Chapter 5. The Return of Christ – What We Shall Be
Chapter 6. The Return of Christ – When He Will Come
Chapter 7. What Jesus Taught
Chapter 8. What the Apostles Taught
Chapter 9. Truth and Deception
Chapter 10. Martin Luther and His 95 Theses
Chapter 11. Daniel
Chapter 12. The Great Whore of Revelation
Chapter 13. Judgment
Chapter 14. Heaven

Preface

Taking The Kingdom was born from a twelve lesson Bible study series I taught at the church where I Pastor, Apostolic Pentecostal Church, Manchester, Tennessee. In the summer of 2020, the Holy Spirit impressed me to develop a Bible study which would give people a working knowledge of sin, the way to salvation and revelation, including the antichrist, the catching away of the saints, and eternity. I felt then, and do still today, that all people need to know the Word of God, have the knowledge that is written in its pages and understand what to expect in this end-time.

While the chapters of this book may seem to be a smattering of various subjects, I simply followed where the Spirit led me. While we do live for Christ by faith, it is necessary to understand, biblically, why we believe what we believe. I contend, for us to get through the end-time, which is quickly approaching, we need to know what to expect and be armored up.

It is my hope this book answers many questions you may have struggled with in your journey.

Sincerely,
Elton F. Chesser

Foreword

What are the origins of sin? What goes on in the unseen? What does the Bible really say about the end-time?

Whether you are a long-time Christian, or you are just starting your journey in God, these subjects are important bedrock questions of the Faith.

In this book, my friend, Pastor Elton F. Chesser, has penned a groundswell of biblical data and explanations to aid in the understanding of these key truths. I have personally heard him preach and teach on basics as well as deep topics, and his gift of teaching allows some of these convoluted discussions to become disentangled to the average reader.

Some theological books try to simply end with the "Amen" at the end of The Book of Revelation, but this work does not. The historical information of the church is delved into, and in chapters 8-10 the reader gets a bird's-eye view of how the core of New Testament Christianity was muddied and muddled into something else.

What I feel he has done is to take hard concepts and to make them approachable and readable, and I count that this is the core of the gospel effort – to take the "Good News" and bring it to people who have never heard it (and, I should note, the Gospel message of salvation is explained in detail in Chapter 8).

If you are picking up this book as a new soul in a church, please read along in the Scriptures quoted, and look them up – trust me, they're there. See it for yourself, that the gospel message is present, and these ideas are there in the Word of God.

If you are a lifelong saint, I guarantee, he will broach a few subject-matters that can stir you to think and to even understand some long-held conundrums of belief.

But either way, enjoy the material and the way he presents it. I found his personal testimonies of healing and miracles (chapter 3) exciting!

One final note: if you are an unbeliever, or if you don't really know WHAT to believe, or who to believe, I challenge you to pray about this book. Read the Scriptures, read the explanations of biblical thoughts and ideas, and just seek God in prayer. I wonder if maybe – just maybe – could God confirm this to you, somehow?!

Miracles do really come true, and maybe they are for you, too!

May God bless you as you read this book.

Joel Revalee, PhD
Full-time Apostolic minister

Chapter One
The Genesis of Evil

"Who told thee that thou wast naked?" Powerful words coming from the Creator of the universe to a man who was acting quite guilty of something. Of course, God knew what had happened, but He needed to have this conversation with Adam. If you read the third chapter of Genesis, you see a pattern that looks quite familiar, even in our day. God asked Adam, "Hast thou eaten of the tree whereof I commanded thee that thou shouldest not eat?"

Adam didn't confess and come clean but rather threw shade on Eve. "The woman whom thou gavest to be with me, she gave me of the tree, and I did eat." A ploy still used by millions to this day. When you're guilty, just throw attention toward someone else and maybe the prosecutors will focus on them.

So, God moves on to Eve. "What is this that thou hast done?" God asks Eve. Eve's immediate response is to point to the serpent. Let's pass the buck if we can. And the woman said, "the serpent beguiled me, and I did eat." God then moves on to the serpent but, rather than hear his excuses, God simply pronounces judgment.

> Genesis 3:14 KJV. "Because thou hast done this, thou art cursed above all cattle, and above every beast of the field, upon thy belly shalt thou go, and dust shalt thou eat all the days of thy life: and I will put enmity between thy seed, and her seed."

No one got away with their sin. The serpent was punished, as was Adam and Eve.

Apostle Paul explained our current spiritual condition from a humanity standpoint.

> Romans 5:12 KJV. “Wherefore as by one man sin entered into the world, and death by sin; and so death passed upon all men, for that all have sinned.”

While Adam was the first man to sin, and so death and sin has now passed to all men (we are born in sin), Adam and Eve were not unique. Neither Adam nor Eve invented sin nor created it. Sin was born long before God formed Adam from the dust of the earth and breathed into his nostrils the breath of life.

We are seeing prophecies come to pass and the world change before our very eyes. It is extremely important, when we study the Word of God, that we understand what we are reading and keep everything in context. When we study the end-time, we need to have proper context. We must rightly divide the Word.

Take a look at Isaiah chapter 14. God is speaking judgment against Babylon and her king on behalf of Israel. In verse 12 God directs His attention to where true sin and evil exists. God moves his attention to Satan himself... Lucifer. God wants us to understand this isn’t just about a bad king doing bad things. There are spirits of evil behind Babylon and her king. It began in Heaven before either Babylon or her king existed.

> Isaiah 14:12-14 KJV. "How art thou fallen from heaven, O Lucifer, son of the morning! How art thou cut down to the ground, which didst weaken the nations! For thou hast said in thine heart, I will ascend into heaven, I will exalt my throne above the stars of God: I will sit also upon the mount of the congregation, in the sides of the north: I will ascend above the heights of the clouds; I will be like the most High."

Nothing good ever comes from Satan. If the enemy speaks to you, he's lying. He's the father of lies. We can certainly see how evil (Satan) has weakened the nations, just as recorded in Isaiah chapter 12.

In the beginning, Lucifer was not evil. He was a created spirit being made by God. Even the name he carries means "light." Lucifer attempted to lift himself to the throne of God. The throne room is God's place. I will ascend above the clouds? I will be like the Most High? No! God says you will be broughtdown.

> Isaiah 14:15 KJV. "Yet thou shalt be brought down to hell, to the sides of the pit."

This is the prophet Isaiah, the one who writes prophecies and future events. The prophet who entered into the very throne room of God, writing about the angelic hosts flying about, praising God, while the pillars shook and smoke filled the room. While writing concerning Babylon, God said, let's address the spirit that causes evil things to happen. I want to speak to the very spirit this comes from. That spirit of the king of Babylon was high and mighty, taking Israel captive, but there was another spirit driving the king. The spirit that was born in the heart of Lucifer some time ago. The spirit that caused Satan himself to be cast from Heaven.

We see this spirit in the world today. We see cities burned down out of hatred, or just for entertainment purposes. We see police, and those in authority, dishonored and disrespected. We need to understand, all these things are deeper than simply anger. There are spirits in the world today: spirits of evil, spirits of hatred, spirits of calamity. These spirits come right from the beginning of time, before Adam, when Lucifer, the shining light, became proud and boasted of what he was going to do. God stepped in and put Lucifer in his place. There would be no need for the things written in the book of Revelation if Lucifer had stayed in his place and honored the Creator.

We need to have a working knowledge of the spirit of darkness that roams in the world today. There would have been no sin in the Garden of Eden if Lucifer had kept his place. There would be no adultery, no fornication, no murder, nor hatred, if Lucifer had simply kept his place. But when Lucifer fell, God stepped in and cast him from the Heavens. Revelation Chapter 12 tells us after the great war with Michael and his angels that Lucifer, who John calls the great dragon, the Devil and Satan, was cast down to earth. And Satan is angry.

Ezekiel chapter 28 is a chapter very similar to Isaiah chapter 14. God, through his prophet Ezekiel, is dealing with the prince of Tyrus. God even compliments him, calling him wiser than Daniel, and with understanding, but tells him his heart is lifted up, and because he has said he is a god, he will die at the hand of strangers. And just as in Isaiah, there is a shift that occurs. In Ezekiel 28 we find the change begin in verse 13.

> Ezekiel 28:13-15 KJV. "Thou hast been in Eden the garden of God, every precious stone was thy covering, the sardis, topaz, and the diamond, the beryl, the onyx, and the jasper, the sapphire, the emerald, and the carbuncle, and gold: the workmanship of thy tabrets and thy pipes was prepared in thee in the day that thou wast created. Thou art the anointed cherub that covereth; and I have set thee so: thou wast upon the holy mountain of God; thou hast walked up and down in the midst of the stones of fire. Thou wast perfect in thy ways from the day thou wast created, till iniquity was found in thee."

Lucifer was anointed. He stood upon the holy mountain of God. He was perfect. Until he wasn't. When iniquity was found in him. What a sad testimony of a created being who seemingly had it all! Who wouldn't want to dwell forever in the Heavens as a servant of the Most High God? For Lucifer, it wasn't enough. And because iniquity or pride entered into his heart, he lost it all.

There is a spirit behind the evil we see in the darkness of the world. There is a spirit behind the pride. There is a spirit in the haughtiness.

God did not create the evil. It came to be from Lucifer's heart. He wanted to be like God. If you think about it, it started with a wrong attitude. Being created in perfection wasn't good enough for Lucifer. But God said, no, it doesn't work that way. From Lucifer's pride and attitude, came violence and war in Heaven and eventually on earth as well.

Picture this... Before God ever created the earth. Before God ever created Adam from the dust of the ground and breathed His own breath into him, giving him a soul, imagine we're in the throne room of God with his created angelic host. Created perfect and anointed by God. Holiness abounds. Then, from somewhere in the reaches of Heaven, one angel proclaims, "This isn't good enough for me. I want to elevate my throne with God."

And when Lucifer was cast from Heaven, he took a third of the angels with him in his rebellion. But even that wasn't good enough for Lucifer. When God created Adam and then Eve, Lucifer cast his eyes on humanity. "If I can't have Heaven, I want earth. If I can't have God's throne room, I'll create my own." No doubt, Lucifer quipped, "I'll spoil God's plan." See how just one misguided desire took the plan and will of God and put it in a spin?

We're not even talking about lost humanity yet. When God would look down from His throne and see that mankind could not even obey ten simple rules, He would decide to robe Himself in flesh and become the Lamb sacrifice that would save humanity, hoping some would accept Him.

We're talking about a war in Heaven of epic proportions that would affect Heaven, earth and eternity.

The word Satan simply means "adversary," or "to oppose." But it has become the term we use for ultimate evil. And even the name, Lucifer, in the beginning wasn't intended to be a term of negativity. But some names have negative connotations because of evil or sin connected to them. One example: Hitler.

Another worthy Scripture on the subject is II Peter 2:4, "For if God spared not the angels that sinned, but cast them down to hell, and delivered them into chains of darkness, to be reserved unto judgement..." God did not even spare the angels that rebelled with Lucifer. So, if God did not even spare those angels who were created perfect and with anointing, don't expect Him to spare us if we do not follow Him. For we are a flawed people, thanks to sin. We are a fallen humanity saved only by the redeeming blood of the Lamb sacrificed on Calvary: resurrected and coming again for a Bride who has made herself ready.

Jude, in his epistle, also speaks of the fallen angels in verse six, "which kept not their first estate, but left their own habitation," stating that God has "reserved in everlasting chains under darkness unto the judgement of the great day."

> Ephesians 6:12 KJV. "For we wrestle not against flesh and blood, but against principalities, against powers, against the rulers of the darkness of this world, against spiritual wickedness in high places."

If we fought against a physical enemy, it would be easier. We would just get the larger weapon, or build the bigger force. But we are fighting against spirits and rulers of darkness in this world. The reason sin hides in darkness is because the enemy does not want us to have the ability to see the wickedness and the price that eventually must be paid. We are fighting spirits of evil that began long before humanity.

When we read the story of the birth of Jesus, it never fails to give us a warm feeling and lift our spirits. The story of a godly young lady who readily accepts the will of God for her life, no matter what. A young man who follows the direction of the angel Gabriel and takes the young woman as his wife. We have angels singing and proclaiming hosannas to the

Highest. It's a totally feel-good story. Every December, we pick out cute little Sunday School children to put on robes and recite the lines. It's a timeless story which brings tears of joy to our eyes and hope to our hearts and lives. But due to the rebellion of Lucifer long before Mary and Joseph were born, there's a dark side to the story as well.

> Revelation 12:1-5 KJV. "And there appeared a great wonder in heaven, a woman clothed with the sun, and the moon under her feet, and upon her head a crown of twelve stars: and she being with child cried, travailing in birth, and pained to be delivered. And there appeared another wonder in heaven, and behold a great red dragon, having seven heads and ten horns, and seven crowns upon his heads. And his tail drew the third part of the stars of heaven and did cast them to the earth: and the dragon stood before the woman, which was ready to be delivered, for to devour her child as soon as it was born. And she brought forth a man child, who was to rule all nations with a rod of iron: and her child was caught up unto God, and to his throne."

Then the Scripture describes a war in heaven with Michael and his angels, and Lucifer and his followers. Lucifer was cast into the world, and this world was deceived. Everyone who knows me, knows that I do not like to give credit to the devil. I believe we often give him much more credit than he deserves. Many of the struggles people face today are due to poor decisions, or lack of desire, not the devil. However, it is true that Satan has spiritual power to fight against the things of God and humanity. He seeks to conquer and destroy. The Apostle John writes about hearing a loud voice in verse ten that tells us theaccuser of the brethren is cast down. He then explains how to overcome the Satan.

> Revelation 12:11 KJV. “And they overcame him by the blood of the Lamb, and by the word of their testimony, and they loved not their lives unto the death.”

There are not many things in this old world worth dying for. But the Name of Jesus Christ, and a life in Him, is one.

Chapter Two
The Spirit World and Calvary

I do believe our greatest struggle is with the person we see each day in the mirror. Because of our fallen nature, we are fighting spirits we cannot see. Many things we watch, see, or involve ourselves with, while on the surface may seem harmless, if we are not mindful, may introduce harmful ideology or spirits into our lives. We may introduce spirits into our homes and families by way of inappropriate television programs, computers, cellphones, and other electronic devices and literature.

> John 13:21-27 KJV. "When Jesus had thus said, he was troubled in spirit, and testified, and said, Verily, verily, I say unto you, that one of you shall betray me. Then the disciples looked one on another, doubting of whom he spake. Now there was leaning on Jesus' bosom one off his disciples, whom Jesus loved. Simon Peter therefore beckoned to him, that he should ask who it should be of whom he spake. He then lying on Jesus' breast saith unto him, Lord, who is it? Jesus answered, He it is, to whom I shall give a sop, when I have dipped it. And when he had dipped the sop he gave it to Judas Iscariot, the son of Simon. And after the sop Satan entered into him. Then said Jesus unto him, That thou doest, do quickly."

See also Luke 22:1-6

Jesus was troubled in His spirit, and rightly so. The Lord is having the last supper with the disciples and says to them, one of you will betray me. The disciples begin to look around at each other wondering, who in his right mind would walk away from the Messiah? Who would throw all this away after following him forty-two months and seeing healings, miracles, and countless people delivered?

After Jesus handed the sop to Judas, Satan entered into him (Judas). See what's happening here? Judas, sitting at the table with the Creator of the universe, the Messiah, the Christ, the Savior of the world, became demon possessed. The enemy is not afraid to enter into our churches and sit among the people of God. He is looking for someone who is not totally committed to the things of God and His ministry. He seeks out the one who is unstable in his dedication.

People give all kinds of reasons and excuses for not living a life in Christ. It's their pastor, or the church leadership. Perhaps a conflict of personalities. Maybe the pastor is too hard, or too soft. And let's not forget about those hypocrites. Oh, I could live a joyously, successful life in Jesus if it weren't for all those hypocrites.

I readily admit that some people and pastors don't match up. There are times a change can honestly help a person have a more successful Christian life. I've actually suggested to a few people in my past to feel free to visit other churches who preach truth and see if they would be happier there. If you can't live for God with me as your pastor, go find a pastor you can live for God with.

The bottom line is, we've got to get to Heaven. That's goal

number one. Of course, the most proven way to live for the Lord and have an overcoming life is having a mind made up. Deny the flesh, and never turn back to the darkness of the world. Ignore the hypocrites, they're everywhere, including work, school, and the grocery store. Most importantly, keep an active life of prayer.

> John 6:66 KJV. "From that time many of his disciples went back and walked no more with him."

If Judas and these many disciples found it too difficult to live for Jesus with Him right there with them, the problem was obviously within their own hearts. Wherever we are, whatever we must do, we have to find a place of total commitment to Christ Jesus. The prize is too great to fail. The prize is Heaven. Let us not allow ourselves to become distracted.

While growing up, I would at times find myself facing a challenge that required all my effort. I had to be totally committed to succeed. I would hear my mother's voice say to me, "Son, jump in with all four feet." She was telling me to give it my all. Be completely committed and don't give any space for failure. To have our robes white and enter Heaven, we must jump in with all four feet.

Evil influences our culture and society. As Christians insist on morality and ethical principles, the world pushes farther and farther to the left. Many times, we are called hateful and judgmental because we stand for what is right and good according to the Word of God. A popular cry for our day is "Don't judge me!"

> John 12:47-48 KJV. "And if any man hear my words, and believe not, I judge him not: for I came not to judge the world, but to save the world. He that rejecteth me, and receiveth not my words, hath one that judgeth him: the word that I have spoken, the same shall judge him in the last day."

It is true, Jesus did not come to judge you, or me. He came to save us. He loves us. He has given us a great deal of teaching and instruction to live by. He promised He would keep us in perfect peace. He has promised healing, deliverance, and salvation. All we must do is believe and receive. He'll even give you the power to live an overcoming life. That's what the Holy Ghost is for.

But, for those who are the "don't judge me" crowd, there is a judgment day coming. Our judge will be the words (instructions) Jesus gave us to live by. I've said it many times over the years. If one could read the entire Bible and then be asked to describe it in one word, to me the word would be "obey." The sure way to Heaven is simply obey. Everything else will fall right into place. Jesus said so. "But seek ye first the kingdom of … righteousness..." (Matthew 6:33).

> Ephesians 6:10-12 KJV. "Finally, my brethren, be strong in the Lord, and in the power of his might. Put on the whole armor of God, that ye may be able to stand against the wiles of the devil. For we wrestle not against flesh and blood, but against the rulers of the darkness of this world, against spiritual wickedness in high places."

There are demonic spirits working all across our world today:

in governments, in school systems, and in society. They are working with rulers who are in high places of power. These are the spirits "everyday people" wrestle against every day. There are many fine people who are leaders, who desire to guide our nation, schools, and military in a direction that they sincerely feel is best. But not all feel this same way. The spirits are working in them who will let them work. Satan used people to betray Jesus and crucify Him. Satan is not above using people to try to destroy you as well. This is why Apostle Paul ordered us to put on the armor of God.

> John 19:28, 30 KJV "After this, Jesus knowing that all things were now accomplished, that the scripture might be fulfilled, saith, I thirst. When Jesus therefore had received the vinegar, he said, it is finished: and he bowed his head, and gave up the ghost."

Hanging on the cross, just before giving up the ghost, Jesus used the Greek word, "tetelesai," which has been translated into English as "it is finished." Tetelesai is an accounting term, which means "paid in full." God manifested Himself into earthly flesh, walked among men, and sacrificed His life on Calvary for the salvation of mankind. As Christ drew His last breath He proclaimed, "It is paid in full." He paid the price for our healing, salvation, and redemption with His death on Calvary. It's finished ... it's Paid In Full!

Of course, I can't talk about Calvary without mentioning what happened three days later. Calvary purchased our healing, our redemption, and salvation, but the resurrection is what gave it all power and victory. Without the resurrection, Calvary would not have mattered. The resurrection was the beginning of a new chapter.

Jesus didn't just lay in a comatose state during those three days in the tomb. He went into the depths of hell and took back the keys to death, hell, and the grave. Jesus had warned them, if you tear down this Temple, I will build it up again in three days. Of course, they didn't understand.

Hanging on the cross, Jesus did not look like the Savior of the world, or the Creator. He looked like a criminal. There are times in our lives when we may not look like a winner. But give yourself and the power of the Holy Ghost time to work. Sometimes we are on a mountain top and sometimes in a valley. Sometimes we're shouting victory, and sometimes we're feeling all alone. There have been times when I was so weak and sick I wondered if I would ever feel good again, or have the strength to get up and work again. I had to give myself time. Strength was coming.

> Hebrews 11:35-38 KJV. "Women received their dead raised to life again: and others were tortured, not accepting deliverance; that they might obtain a better resurrection: and others had trial of cruel mockings and scourgings, yea, moreover of bonds and imprisonment: they were stoned, they were sawn asunder, were tempted, were slain with the sword: they wandered about in sheepskins and goatskins; being destitute, afflicted, tormented; (of whom the world was not worthy) they wandered in deserts, and in mountains, and in dens and caves of the earth."

These people were victorious!

When Jesus fasted forty days, He did not try to come to an agreement with Satan. With Judas, Jesus did not try to work out some agreement or talk him out of fulfilling his plan of betraying the Messiah for thirty pieces of silver. Jesus told Judas, whatever you're doing, go do it. Let's get it done. Jesus knew in just a few hours He would be hanging on a cross. He did not come to compromise. I'm not a big fan of boxing, but I have learned this about the sport over the years. When those two big muscle guys get into the ring, they're not interested in making nice, or becoming friends. They have one goal. Knock the other guy out before he knocks me out. There's no compromise. Jesus did not come to compromise.

One of my favorite passages of Scripture is found in Revelation chapter one. John is in the Spirit, possibly praying or worshipping. He hears this voice speaking to him from behind. Hearing this voice behind him, he turns to see who it is. He describes the individual and realizes it's Jesus. Now remember, John has not seen Jesus face to face in over sixty years. The experience was so overwhelming for John that he passes out, right at the feet of Jesus. Here's the part I love. Jesus reaches down and lays His right hand on His old friend, John. John comes to himself enough to hear what Jesus says next.

> Revelation 1:17,18 KJV "Fear not; I am the first and the last: I am he that liveth, and was dead; and behold, I am alive for evermore, Amen; and have the keys of hell and of death."

In this human, fleshly existence, we still experience death. Our bodies still grow old, and we will come to an earthy demise because our flesh is corruptible. The resurrection is proof of ultimate victory. Jesus has given us the victory.

> I Corinthians 15:51-55 KJV. "Behold I shew you a mystery; We shall not all sleep, but

we shall all be changed, in a moment, in the twinkling of an eye, at the last trump: for the trumpet shall sound, and the dead shall be raised incorruptible, and we shall be changed. For this corruptible must put on incorruption, and this mortal must put on immortality. So, when this corruptible shall have put on incorruption, and this mortal shall have put on immortality, then shall be brought to pass the saying that is written, Death is swallowed up in victory. O death, where is thy sting? O grave, where is thy victory?"

Chapter Three
The Birth of the Church Age

> Acts 2:1-4 KJV. "And when the day of Pentecost was fully come, they were all with one accord in one place. And suddenly there came a sound from heaven as of a rushing mighty wind, and it filled all the house where they were sitting. And there appeared unto them cloven tongues like as of fire, and it sat upon each of them. And they were all filled with the Holy Ghost, and began to speak with other tongues, as the Spirit gave them utterance."

If we find it difficult to live victoriously for the Lord now, when His Spirit is moving in our churches and working in our lives, how are we ever going to live for Him when we go through trials or temptations or in these last days as we draw closer to the end-time and time of tribulation. We need to grab hold now, very strongly, making up our minds and live for Him wholly and completely while we live in the church age where we have the blessing and benefit of healings, miracles, and the outpouring of the Holy Ghost.

Acts chapter two describes the birth of the church. These people were not just born again by modern definition, which falls short, but they experienced the birth of the church. Enter the Church Age. We are still currently in the Church

Age. Just as the Holy Ghost fell upon people in Acts chapters 2, 8, 10, and 19, it still falls on people today, changing lives and redeeming spirits.

The "Day of Pentecost" was the Feast of First Fruits, described in Exodus. Luke refers to it as Pentecost, given the Greek influence during the time of Christ. This was one of the three festivals, when the men of Israel were to return to Jerusalem. It occurred fifty days after the Passover. Because of this feast, the temple and streets of Jerusalem were filled with good, godly Hebrew men. How's that for God's timing?

Apostle John recorded in chapter 20 of his Gospel account, Jesus breathed on the apostles and told them to "receive the Holy Ghost." The Lord told them there would be signs which would follow them that believe. "In my name shall they cast out devils; they shall speak with new tongues; they shall take up serpents; and if they drink any deadly thing, it shall not hurt them; they shall lay hands on the sick, and they shall recover" (Mark 16:17,18).

After instructing them on other topics, and opening their understanding so they could understand the Scripture (no doubt Jesus definitely wanted them to understand what to teach and preach), Jesus instructed them to tarry in Jerusalem until they be "endued with power from on high" (Luke 24:49).

> Acts 1:8 KJV. "But ye shall receive POWER,
> after that the Holy Ghost is come upon you..."

What is this power of the Holy Ghost, and where does He come from? Jesus sought to explain this phenomenon to the apostles.

> John 14:16-18 KJV. "And I will pray the Father, and he shall give you another Comforter, that he may abide with you forever, even the Spirit of truth; whom the world cannot receive, because it seeth him not, neither knoweth him: but ye know him, for he dwelleth with you, and shall be in you. I will not leave you comfortless. I will come to you."

There they were, sitting, praying, and worshipping in the upper room. When the Holy Ghost fell, they were in one accord. They were in unity of spirit and purpose. God will not move in a church that is not in unity. He may move on some of the faithful, but the demonstration and power of the Holy Ghost will be limited by the disunity overall. It's difficult to have revival and win new souls to Christ when the body of believers is divided.

The Jewish men who were in the temple and Jerusalem for the Feast of Weeks, or day of Pentecost, as Luke called it, had no idea what was happening in that upper room and began to gather round. One hundred twenty people were speaking in tongues simultaneously as the Spirit gave them utterance. Some must have been staggering, falling, or displaying other physical behavior that seemed quite unusual, because the men who had gathered thought these Disciples of Christ were drunk. As Peter attempted to answer their questions and explain what was happening, he no doubt remembered an Old Testament Scripture he had read many times.

> Joel 2:28,29 KJV. "And it shall come to pass afterward, that I will pour out my spirit upon all flesh; and your sons and your daughters shall prophesy, your old men shall dream

> dreams, your young men shall see visions: and also upon the servants and upon the handmaids in those days will I pour out my spirit."

The part of Peter's message that gets me every time is Acts 2:36, "Therefore let all the house of Israel know assuredly, that God hath made that same Jesus, whom ye have crucified, both Lord and Christ."

Wait a minute, what? WE killed the Lord and Christ? We did? Verse 37 tells us the men were pricked in their hearts. It hurt their spirits. They couldn't take it. NO... we killed the Lord, the Christ? The Messiah? Then they asked the question Peter and the other apostles were no doubt waiting for and welcomed. "Men and brethren, what shall we do?" I love it when people make it easy and simply ask. What do I need to do to be saved? I love Peter's response. He put it in a nice little package, with the steps in order, so anyone could understand. Let's break down Peter's response in verse 38.

What to do?... Repent and be baptized
Who?... Every one of you
How?... in the Name of Jesus Christ
Why?... for the remission of sins
Reward... and ye shall receive the gift of the Holy Ghost

Then in verse 39, Peter explained that the promise is "for you, your children, and to all that are afar off, even as many as the Lord our God shall call." He called it a promise. When people make promises one to another, many times the promises are broken. We human beings aren't quite as reliable as we would like to think. But when the Lord makes a promise, He keeps His Word. Some promises God makes to us in His Word are unconditional. Meaning, it doesn't matter what you do or what you think about it. God said it, so He's going to do it for you.

Other promises in the Word of God are conditional. To receive the promise of the Holy Ghost, we have certain steps we must accomplish. We must believe He is who He says He is, and we must seek Him. If a person truly repents of their sin and is baptized in Jesus' Name, and continues to seek the Lord, He will fill you with the promise of the Holy Ghost.

> Jeremiah 29:13 KJV. "And ye shall seek me, and find me, when ye shall search for me with all your heart."

When Peter finished his message, and the crowd indeed heard what they needed to do, 3,000 were baptized that same day in the Name of Jesus Christ for the remission of their sins.

"And they continued steadfastly in the apostles' doctrine and fellowship, and in breaking bread, and in prayers" (verse 42). After we come to the knowledge of the power of the Holy Ghost and experience it ourselves, we must continue in those things, and especially prayer.

The church in the book of Acts, after the Holy Ghost fell upon them in the second chapter, was a church of healings, miracles, and deliverances. Our churches today should greatly resemble the book of Acts church. It should be a common occurrence for us to experience healings in our church services. In our churches, when someone is delivered from drugs, alcohol, or any other type of worldly bondage, it should not come as a surprise to us, but rather it should be the norm.

When Peter reached for the hand of the lame man in Acts chapter three, to lift him to his feet, his legs and feet immediately received strength. He leaped and praised God with Peter and John. The very shadow of Peter, as he walked through the streets of Jerusalem, cast healing upon those who were sick and afflicted. Apostle Paul's ministry was so powerful, people began to seek cloths and pieces of material from him to send to loved ones for healing.

Obviously, the power of healing and deliverance didn't come from these men themselves, nor their clothing. The power came from the Holy Ghost that dwelt in them. They were simply the vessels God used. All healings, power, deliverance, and the infilling of the Holy Ghost comes from Jesus Himself. We need to position ourselves spiritually to be used by the Spirit at any given moment in time.

Many years ago, while pastoring in Missouri, I received a call one evening from one of the ladies from the church. She was married and she and her husband had three children, the youngest being a boy about three years old at the time, named David. She told me how David had been running a fever all day and was extremely sick. She was quite concerned and asked if I would come to pray for David. When I stepped into their living room, I saw David across the room lying on the sofa. He was indeed sickly looking and was quite lethargic.

After exchanging pleasantries with the parents, I began to step across the room to David. David's mom warned me, Pastor, please watch out for all the cars and trucks and toys scattered across the floor. I brought them in earlier today trying to get David to play, but he hasn't played or eaten all day long, she explained. I leaned over this little boy to explain what I was about to do before I touched him.

"David", I said, "I'm going to lay my hand on you and pray for you that the Lord will heal you, OK?" David nodded his little head and was able to grunt out an affirmative response. When I laid my hand across David's forehead to pray for him, I could feel the intense heat of his fever. I have no idea how high this little boy's fever was, but I can say I've never felt a fever this hot since that day. I began to pray a simple prayer, and I could hear the parents praying behind me.

I'm not one to shake a person or push and shove them while praying. I realize the power of healing and deliverance isn't in how hard you shake a person around, it's all in the power of the Name of Jesus. Isaiah told us we're healed by the stripes that were beaten into the body of Jesus at Calvary. He really doesn't need anything more from me than to be a vessel He can use.

As I was praying for David, I began to feel the most amazing thing. I could feel under my hand the fever subsiding. With every word of my prayer, I could feel David's temperature descending downward. By the time I finished my prayer with, "In Jesus Name, Amen," I could tell David's body temperature was normal.

As I lifted my hand off David's forehead, he immediately leaped from the sofa and grabbed a couple of the cars that had been lying on the floor all day, begging to be played with. "Vrooom Vrooom," David exclaimed as he raced two of the cars across the floor in front of the sofa. By this time the family members were amazed and rejoicing.

At that moment David looked up at his mother who was standing over him and said, "Momma, I'm huuungreeee." I'll never forget the way he said it. We couldn't help but laugh while giving Jesus the glory. I explained to the family how I had felt David's fever go down under my hand as we were praying. We continued to rejoice as momma went to the kitchen to fix David a late supper.

> Isaiah 53:5 KJV. "But he was wounded for our transgressions, he was bruised for our iniquities; the chastisement of our peace was upon him; and with his stripes we are healed."
>
> Psalm 9: 1,2 KJV. "I will praise thee, O Lord, with my whole heart; I will shew forth all thy marvelous works. I will be glad and rejoice in thee. I will sing praise to thy name, O thou Most High."

In the tenth chapter of the book of Acts, we see what appears to be an aberration. God speaks to Cornelius, who was a good man. He loves God, gives money to help the poor, and he has an active prayer life. But we find the angel of the Lord visits Cornelius and instructs him to send to Joppa for Apostle Peter, who Cornelius does not know, and has never met.

As the men, who Cornelius sent to Joppa to find Peter, approach the house, Peter is on the roof top praying. But he has fallen into a trance, or a vision. God directs Peter to go with these men without questioning. When Peter and the six other Jewish men who traveled with him make it to Caesarea and enter Cornelius' house, they find the place full of his family, other relatives, servants, and soldiers. After a brief conversation between the two men, Peter, realizing that he had been sent there by God to preach to Cornelius and his family the Gospel message, begins to tell all about Jesus, His life, His teachings, and the Comforter.

Suddenly, to Peter's amazement, the Holy Ghost fell on all of them in the house, who happened to be Gentiles. How did Peter know the Holy Ghost had fallen on Gentiles?

> Acts 10: 45-46 KJV. "And they of the circumcision which believed were astonished, as many as came with Peter, because that on the Gentiles also was poured out the gift of the Holy Ghost. For they heard them speak with tongues and magnify God."

Hearing and seeing that God had now given the Holy Ghost to the Gentiles, just as He had given to the 120 in the upper room, Peter knew the next step was to baptize them in the Name of Jesus Christ.

> Acts 10:47 KJV. "Can any man forbid water, that these should not be baptized, which have received the Holy Ghost as well as we? And he commanded them to be baptized in the Name of the Lord."

The Holy Ghost is for whosoever will seek Him and receive it.

In 1933, there was a couple named Freeman and E.B. Swinford, who lived in southern, middle Tennessee. They had five children at the time but would eventually have ten children, which would produce 34 grandchildren.

The Swinfords heard there was a Pentecostal preacher who had come to the area, and he was holding an old-time brush arbor meeting. This young couple weren't bad people. As a matter of fact, they lived back in the day when even people who didn't go to church had morals and taught their children to do right.

The Swinfords went to that old brush arbor meeting, and there they found something that would change the course of their lives and the lives of their children and grandchildren. In one of those services, E.B. sought after the Lord, and she was filled with the Holy Ghost with the evidence of speaking in tongues, just as in the book of Acts. They were both baptized, and a few months later Freeman received the Holy Ghost as well.

The years have gone by and both Freeman and E.B. have gone on to their reward, but many of their descendants live for Jesus in victory, and several ministers have come up after them in the family. It all started when a young couple attended an old brush arbor meeting with hungry hearts for God.

Freeman and E.B. were my grandparents, and child number four was my mother. I'm very thankful for this heritage and being raised knowing what the power of the Holy Ghost can do in someone's life.

We dare not receive, believe, or teach any other doctrine than the one given to the apostles by Jesus, which the apostles carried on in the book of Acts and in their Epistles. The church that Christ built with His own blood on Calvary, and the power of His resurrection, demands the demonstration of the Holy Ghost. Let us live in the power of the Holy Ghost.

> Galatians 1:8,9 KJV. "But though we, or an angel from heaven, preach any other gospel unto you than that which we have preached unto you, let him be accursed. As we said before, so say I now again, if any man preach

> any other gospel unto you than that ye have received, let him be accursed."
>
> I Corinthians 2:4 KJV. "And my speech and my preaching was not with enticing words of man's wisdom, but in demonstration of the Spirit and of power."

Welcome to the Church Age!

Chapter 4
God's Timing

I will be the first to admit, I don't always understand God's timing. There have been times in my life that God answered a prayer that I had not yet even prayed, and there have been times I prayed with such great faith and conviction I knew God would answer, and yet things dragged on and on. During those times I had no idea what God was waiting on, or why.

While pastoring in Chicago several years ago, I became very ill one February. I went to bed on a Sunday night after church service feeling fine, and awakened Monday morning feeling very fatigued and just not well. I couldn't put my finger on it, but something was wrong.

After struggling for three days, I finally made an appointment with my doctor. I didn't know it at the time, but this was the beginning of a seven-month struggle that would baffle many doctors and leave me greatly incapacitated. From February into October, I struggled to work, pastor the church, and just keep a normal routine.

I could feel the fatigue beginning to strike, and I would be in bed for two or three days, too weak to get up and even shave my face.

During that time, I prayed with greater faith than I had ever prayed. I had seen God heal many people through prayer, and I saw no reason for my illness to be any different. I had been healed instantaneously a number of times in the past, so

I had no trouble believing the Lord could do another miracle in my life, yet this mystery illness continued to attack my body.

Toward the end of summer, I and others began to hear about this illness that seemed to strike younger people who lived mostly in urban areas. They called it the yuppie disease. My mother actually found an article about this little-known illness in a popular magazine at the time and called me one day telling me I needed to read it.

When my folks drove into the city for Bible study that Wednesday night, Mom brought the magazine with the article. As I read this news article, I found I was reading about myself: the fatigue, the symptoms, the struggle. It was as though the writer of this news piece had been spying on me and wrote about it.

I began to search the city of Chicago for a specialist who I could see to get some answers. I found a doctor at St. Luke's Presbyterian Medical Center who had an opening, and I made an appointment. The scheduler I spoke with told me to write down all my symptoms and bring the list. The day finally arrived, and I walked into the specialist's office with a list of thirteen various symptoms that I had struggled with at one time or another. At this point I had been sick more than seven months.

That day I was diagnosed with Chronic Fatigue Syndrome. I got a little excited just having a name attached to this horrible illness that had plagued me for so long. "Now what do we do?" I asked. "How do we treat this?" The doctor looked dejected, dropped his eyes and said, "Unfortunately, there's nothing we can do. We don't know what causes this and there's no cure. The best we can do is treat the symptoms."

My excitement turned to disappointment.

I drove home that day, discouraged. Lord, I said in my heart, if I was going to have an incurable disease that I would have to live with for the rest of my life, I think I'd rather have one that would just kill me. I was only 30 years old at the time, and I figured I had decades of this illness to contend with unless I could receive healing. I knew God was, and is, a healer. I had received healing many times, and I had seen God heal many people. Why wasn't I receiving healing this time?

I had an appointment to see this specialist again in three weeks. In the meantime, I hit a spell of insomnia that about wore me out. In eight nights, I was able to sleep only fifteen hours. I was weak and miserable. I devised a plan on Saturday evening that I hoped would work. If I could stay up late on Saturday night, until I was so sleepy I couldn't take it any longer, maybe I could then fall into bed and go right to sleep. That would hopefully give me enough rest to be able to be in church Sunday morning with my congregation, and I could preach the message. I did just that and when I was so sleepy I could hardly stay awake, I slipped into bed. I tossed and turned for almost two hours trying to go to sleep. Finally, around 12:30 that Sunday morning, I rolled over onto my stomach and propped myself up on my elbows, burying my face in my hands. "God," I said, "You called me to this church. You called me to reach the lost and lead these people. But I cannot do it unless You heal me." I had prayed this prayer with the same amount of faith for seven months. Nothing really had changed in my heart or faith. I didn't realize it, but I was waiting on God's timing.

After I prayed this prayer, that I had no doubt prayed several times that summer, I felt a tingling sensation in my torso. I felt an actual physical, real tingling inside my body. This tingling sensation continued for about thirty seconds and stopped. When it did, I felt different. I can't really explain it, other than I felt "different." I realized the Lord had just healed me of that horrible, exhausting sickness that had plagued me, my family, and my church for months. I climbed out of bed and while patting my body up and down, I rhetorically asked the Lord, "You just healed me didn't you!?!? You just healed me!"

The apartment was on the third floor, so I excitedly made my way to the church sanctuary which was on the second floor. For two and a half hours I stood, walked, and marched around the altar of the church, praising God and giving Him thanks. After that time of rejoicing and thankfulness, I went back upstairs, climbed into bed, and immediately fell asleep for the first time in more than a week.

When the alarm awakened me in the morning, I jumped out of bed with great anticipation. Ten o'clock church time could not get here fast enough. Finally, with the musicians at their instruments, and the congregation in the pews waiting to begin worship, I started church that morning by announcing, "at 12:30 this morning while lying in bed praying, God completely and totally healed me of that sickness."

The reaction of the church was just as you are thinking at this moment. There were hands raised in thanks, shouts of praise, and some tears of joy. There was excitement in the church that we really needed to see. We knew the Lord could heal. We had known that the entire time, but now it had happened. God can do anything. Nothing is impossible with him.

About the same time, I had scheduled a Sunday night revival service with a minister whom I had never met. He grew up in

Chicago and moved to the Los Angeles area. After moving to California, he came to know truth, was baptized in Jesus' Name, and received the Holy Ghost with the evidence of speaking in tongues. He was coming to our church to give his testimony. He invited many family members and friends to come hear him. That Sunday night, which was four weeks after my healing, he arrived to preach and give his testimony.

That evening twenty-four visitors, whom he had invited, walked in for the service. When he gave the altar call, ten of those twenty-four came to the altar. Three received the Holy Ghost and several repented. One of the visitors was delivered from a horrible drug addiction he had been battling. Several were baptized, and from that one service, I started five Exploring God's Word Home Bible Studies. Over the course of the next eleven months, we baptized 49 people and 39 received the baptism of the Holy Ghost with the evidence of speaking in other tongues.

I looked back, in the midst of the revival God had brought to us, and realized why I had not been healed until the second Sunday of October. It was all about God's timing.

> Malachi 3:1 KJV. "Behold, I will send my messenger, and he shall prepare the way before me: and the Lord, whom ye seek, shall suddenly come to his temple, even the messenger of the covenant, whom ye delight in: behold, he shall come, saith the Lord of hosts."

God ended the Old Testament with a prophecy and a promise!

After Malachi wrapped up his writings, God did not speak to Israel for four hundred years. No prophets, no prophecies.

Silence. Israel, happy to be back in the promised land after being carried away and held in captivity by Babylon and Syria, for a number of years sought to get back into the rhythm of living. They had the law, the priests, and sacrifices, and so they moved forward. But there was no voice of God speaking to them either directly or indirectly through men of God.

Then one typical day as Zacharias the High Priest, who happened to be childless, was performing his duties at the temple, lighting the incense, something very unusual occurred. Zacharias turned to find an angel of God standing on the right side of the altar of incense. Luke records in his Gospel that when Zacharias saw the angel of God standing nearby, fear fell upon him.

Have you ever noticed in the Word of God, whenever anyone has seen an angel of God it scares them? I must admit, I find this rather amusing. Seems the angel in every occurrence had to tell the poor human, don't be afraid. I've seen some miraculous things in my life. I have even felt the presence of angels in church services worshipping with the saints of God, enjoying the same presence we as humans enjoy. But I've never actually, visually, seen an angel, so I suppose I need to give Zacharias and all the others a break here. Having never experienced this, I'm not quite certain I wouldn't respond in kind with all of them.

Now consider this... God has not spoken to the children of Israel in four hundred years. He has had nothing to say to His people other than what they had already received. Then, suddenly there appears this angel in the temple, in a very holy place, to have a private conversation with the High Priest. The first words God speaks to his people after four hundred years of silence is, "Fear not," (Luke 1: 13).

You're probably familiar with the story. Zacharias can't come to believe what the angel is pronouncing, and so, he loses his ability to speak until many months later when his son is finally born. While the family is trying to decide what the child should be named, Zacharias is finally able to get the words out. His name is John!! John? There's not a single person in our entire family named John. Why John? Because the Lord sent an angel.

That same angel, Gabriel by name, made his way to a young lady by the name of Mary, and once again had to use the term, "fear not." The saying of the angel troubled Mary, but after a chat with Gabriel, she proclaimed, "Behold the handmaid of the Lord; be it unto me according to thy word…" (Luke 1:38). Mary was troubled, and maybe somewhat concerned about what all this meant, but she was steadfast in her desire to be in the perfect will of God.

I can't explain why God was silent for four hundred years, not speaking to Israel, or sending a prophet. I learned a long time ago not to question God's methods, ways, or will. But in His time, He sent forth His angel to declare to a few what the plan now was. After centuries of Israel just living life, God was coming to the temple.

God's timing...

Why do we worry? Do you think God is worried? I don't think He's worried at all. About anything. He's not stressed either. Not one bit. He is sitting on His throne in Heaven with His foot on His foot stool (earth), and He's totally relaxed. He has a plan, and it's all according to His timing. As the people of God, baptized in His Name, filled with His Spirit, we should not be worried or stressed about this life or this world. If we truly believe the Word of God and the plan of

God, we should understand He has everything under control.

Now, if we're not a believer or not filled with His Spirit, we of course need to do something about it. Submit to His will and live a life pleasing to Him. I can't help but imagine, when we worry needlessly, we probably annoy Him. *Insert nervous chuckle here.*

Let us not become frustrated with the Lord, or the will of the Lord, if His timing is not our timing. When we don't understand the timing of God, let us spend our time praising Him. Let's not rush Him or push Him, let us trust Him. Definitely, do not take matters into your own hands to force something to happen or try to manipulate a certain outcome. I can guarantee that won't work out to your favor.

- It was not a coincidence that Simeon and Anna, the prophetess, were in the temple the day Mary and Joseph brought baby Jesus in to be circumcised. It was God's timing.
- It was not a coincidence that the Samaritan woman arrived at the well while Jesus was waiting there for His apostles. It was God's timing.
- It was not a coincidence that Lazarus died while Jesus was out of town. It was God's timing.
- It was not a coincidence that Judas betrayed Jesus the night of the Passover. It was God's timing.
- It was not a coincidence that the repentant thief was hanged on the cross the very same day as the Messiah. It was God's timing.
- It was not a coincidence that the Holy Ghost fell on the one hundred twenty on the exact Day of Pentecost, when God knew thousands of Israelites would be crowded into the temple and the streets of Jerusalem for the feast. It was God's timing.

I could go on and on but by now you get the idea. Let us not wrestle with God concerning things we think should happen in a given time. Our job is to live a victorious, godly life for Christ. If we take care of our business, God will take care of His.

Christ also has an appointed time to return for his bride, the church. He's coming for people who have prepared themselves and made themselves ready. It's in His timing. Let us do what we must do to be prepared and ready.

All of this is going to happen in God's timing!

Chapter 5
The Return of Christ What We Shall Be

Whenever we discuss the Rapture of the church, or the return of Christ for His Bride, we need to understand first of all, that no man knows the day nor the hour when Christ shall appear. We have Scriptures we can cross reference and compare, but the Lord has left this topic fuzzy enough that no man can put an exact finger on it. The important thing is to be ready when He comes. Prepare yourself for that amazing day. Concerning when He'll return, we'll talk more about that in a later chapter. In this chapter I want to discuss what will occur in us and to us when that trumpet sounds.

> I Thessalonians 4:15-18 KJV. "For this we say unto you by the word of the Lord, that we which are alive and remain unto the coming of the Lord shall not prevent them which are asleep. For the Lord himself shall descend from heaven with a shout, with the voice of the archangel, and with the trump of God: and the dead in Christ shall rise first: then we which are alive and remain shall be caught up together with them in the clouds, to meet the Lord in the air: and so shall we ever be with the Lord. Wherefore comfort one another with these words. "

During the time of the earthly ministry of Jesus and beyond, there was a disagreement concerning the resurrection of the dead. The Pharisees, with all their problems of hypocrisy and condescending attitudes, at least believed in the resurrection of the dead. That is to say, they did believe there would be a resurrection and folks would be raised to life again. On the other hand, we have the Sadducees who believed when you die, that's pretty much it. If you passed on, you simply missed out.

Apostle Paul felt the need to address this erroneous doctrine and did so in his letter to the church in Thessalonica. He said what I'm about to tell you, I'm telling you by the Word of the Lord. Those of us who are still alive at the coming of the Lord will not prevent them, or stop them, who are already dead. As a matter of fact, Paul continued, the dead in Christ are going to rise first. Not only are we not going to block them (Chesser paraphrased), or enjoy the resurrection without them, but they will rise first from their graves and head toward the Lord Jesus ahead of us. Then those of us who happen to be alive will go up, and we'll meet them in the air with the Lord. And oh, by the way, there will be shouting, the voice of an archangel, and trumpets. Let's not forget the trumpets.

Paul was basically wanting them to stop worrying about those who have died in Christ. The Lord Jesus isn't going to forget them when He returns. He then encouraged them to comfort one another about this issue. Everything is going to be alright. Just be ready.

> I Corinthians 15:50-55 KJV. "Now this I say brethren, that flesh and blood cannot inherit the kingdom of God; neither doth corruption inherit incorruption. Behold, I shew you a mystery: We shall not all sleep, but we shall

> all be changed, in a moment, in the twinkling of an eye, at the last trump, for the trumpet shall sound, and the dead shall be raised incorruptible, and we shall be changed. For this corruptible must put on incorruption, and this mortal must put on immortality. So when this corruptible shall have put on incorruption, and this mortal shall have put on immortality, then shall be brought to pass the saying that is written, Death is swallowed up I victory. O death, where is thy sting? O grave, where is thy victory?"

I love this passage of Scripture in I Corinthians. I'm looking for the day when I can shed this corrupt, no-good flesh of mine. I want you to notice Paul made it clear, no flesh or blood can inherit the Kingdom of God. If we're going to get through the gates of Heaven, we're going to have to be changed. That change will be from flesh to spirit. We will have spirit bodies in Heaven just as Christ and the angels do.

Here are five points from I Corinthians 15 that Paul made, that I want you to see.

1. Flesh and blood cannot enter into the Kingdom. Neither can bone, since it's part of our flesh. Heaven is going to be a spirit world, just as it is now. Heaven is not going to be changed, we are.
2. Paul said, let me show you a mystery. There are parts of the resurrection, the catching away of the Bride, and new Jerusalem that are mysteries. I believe the Lord intended it to be that way. Paul wrote, "...eye hath not seen, nor ear heard, neither have entered into the heart of man the things which God hath prepared for them that love Him"

(I Corinthians 2:9). Heaven is going to be more magnificent than you've ever imagined.

3. Not all will be dead at Christ's return. Some of us will be alive, carrying on the work of God when He comes.
4. The return of Christ, and the catching away of His Bride, are going to happen so quickly, it will be over before people even realize it's happening. How fast is a twinkling of an eye?
5. Mortal must put on immortality, corruptible must put on incorruption. We will leave all limitations behind. We will leave behind all our illnesses, sicknesses, pain, losses, sadness, depression, and the like to enter a Kingdom where these negative things that weighed us down for years will not exist.

> John 4:23-24 KJV. (Jesus speaking) "But the hour cometh, and now is, when the true worshippers shall worship the Father in spirit and in truth: for the Father seeketh such to worship him. God is a Spirit: and they that worship him must worship him in spirit and in truth."

Let me see if I can break down what Jesus has said here without reading more into it than He intended. First, God is a Spirit. He is deity. God is omniscient, omnipresent, and omnipotent. There is no limit to Him whatsoever. If we are going to worship Him effectively, we must worship Him from our spirit: that spirit that is deep down within each of us. Our soul, if you will.

We've heard of people worshiping in church or praying and it is said, their heart isn't in it. When we're simply going through the motions, or our minds are on other things, we're really not truly worshiping God, are we? True worship comes from our spirit, our soul. True worship begins deep in our heart where we can feel it and show it and mean it. That's the type of worship that moves Heaven.

The beautiful thing about true worship is when we are worshiping from the depth of our heart, our physical being will follow the lead. This is what causes us to raise our hands in worship, clap in praise, and even weep under the presence of God. True worship will save our eternal spirit and affect, or change, our fleshly being.

> Genesis 2:7 KJV. "And the Lord God formed man of the dust of the ground, and breathed into his nostrils the breath of life, and man became a living soul."

We are not fleshly beings on a spiritual journey. We are spiritual beings on a fleshly journey.

Years ago, while pastoring in Chicago, we were enjoying a mighty move of God on a particular Sunday night. Although I could not see them with my natural eyes, while standing in the pulpit, I could feel angels of God flooding the sanctuary, praising the Lord with us. I could feel their presence, and I knew they were there. The glory of God was thick in the building. People were singing and worshiping, the Holy Ghost was falling, and as pastor, I was just letting it go so we could all enjoy the presence of the Savior of the world together.

After a bit, I stepped to the microphone and proclaimed, "I feel the presence of the angels of God in this place with us. They're here worshiping the Lord with us." I noticed one of our musicians begin to cry. I really didn't think much about it, but I did notice it. After church service had ended and we were dismissed, this sister said to me, "When you mentioned the angels of God were in the sanctuary worshiping with us, did you notice I began to cry?" I said, "Yes, I noticed, but I didn't know why." She said, "When I was in the prayer room before church, I asked the Lord to send his angels down to our service to worship with us. When you said what you did from the pulpit, it was confirmation to me that the Lord heard my prayer and answered."

True worship begins in our spirit.

Before I leave this chapter concerning what is going to happen to us when Jesus returns, let me encourage you to prepare yourself for that day. A twinkling of an eye is just a small fraction of a second. That is not enough time to pray and repent. As I stated earlier, it's going to be over before we even realize it's happened!

There was a time in my life when I was a cyclist. I had a nice bike built for speed, and it was a joy to ride. Being built for speed, it was tall and stiff. It was built to go straight and fast, with little variance. I always told myself if I ever find myself about to crash, I'll simply throw my gloved hands in front of myself and break the fall. No big deal.

The day came when I hit a curb, and that tall stiff bike quickly began to pitch forward, and me with it. I had prepared for this day. All I have to do is throw my hands up, protect my face and head (thank God I was wearing a helmet), and do anything else I can to protect myself. As I was thrown over the handlebars, 'This is going to hurt' raced through my mind. I landed on concrete on my head and face, jamming my neck, realizing I had absolutely no time to throw my hands up.

This fail-proof plan I had in my mind all those years was a farce. After an emergency room visit, a few days off work, and a month for the road rash on my face to heal, I was good as new. Lesson learned. This is the way the coming of the Lord is going to be. All the plans for last moment repentance and forgiveness and getting life right are nothing more than an ill-planned farce. Whatever you need to do to be ready for the coming of Jesus, do it now!

"Watch therefore: for ye know not what hour your Lord doth come." (Jesus)

Chapter 6
The Return of Christ When He Will Come

I've heard it preached and taught that Christ is not returning for individuals, but rather his bride, the church. While I suppose that's technically true, I'm listening for the sound of the trump of God and the shout of the archangel. This has got to be a very personal thing for us. For everyone. I am listening and watching. Based upon what's happening in the world, I'm getting more excited as I see the day approaching. As far as I'm concerned, He's coming for me. I must be ready.

> Daniel 12:1-4 KJV. "And at that time shall Michael stand up, the great prince which standeth for the children of thy people: and there shall be a time of trouble, such as never was since there was a nation even to that same time: and at that time thy people shall be delivered, every one that shall be found written in the book. And many of them that sleep in the dust of the earth shall awake, some to everlasting life, and some to shame and everlasting contempt."

Some six hundred years before Christ, and more than two thousand five hundred years before our time, Daniel gave a grave description of the return of Christ, and the resurrection of the Saints. Daniel 12:1-4 is no doubt the clearest description given in the Old Testament prophecy concerning the rapture of the church. In verse five Daniel states "knowledge shall be increased." This is no doubt a description of the day in which we live.

Years ago, there was little technology to be had. As knowledge increased over time, we were able to enjoy items such as cameras, audio recorders, telephones, and even televisions. Computers were introduced, video recorders with built-in audio, and other gadgets came along as knowledge continued to increase. Still a distinct and separate device was needed for all these electronic devices to be used. Today not only are all these electronic devices compacted into one device, but it's all digital and so easy to understand that children can be left to play for hours, although I don't recommend that. And we can hold every bit of it in the palm of our hand.

I will admit to you up front, that some of what I say in this chapter may not sound very encouraging to you. There are some pastors or teachers who won't even approach Revelation, the Tribulation, or the end-time, because it's not a feel-good message. But I firmly believe we need to have knowledge of the end-time to be better prepared.

If we are baptized in the Name of Jesus and filled with His Spirit, we've got nothing to be concerned about except maybe a little inconvenience before we get to enjoy our eternal home in Heaven.

> Matthew 24:29-31 KJV. "Immediately after the tribulation of those days shall the sun be darkened, and the moon shall not give her light, and the stars shall fall from heaven, and the powers of the heavens shall be shaken: and then shall appear the sign of the Son of man in heaven: and then shall all the tribes of

> the earth mourn, and they shall see the Son of man coming in the clouds of heaven with power and great glory. And he shall send his angels with a great sound of a trumpet, and they shall gather together his elect from the four winds, from one end of heaven to the other,"

I may cross your theology here, but what I hear Jesus describing is the tribulation and the return of Christ in glory with his angels, calling the Saints of God home. Some feel He's giving some rundown of Jewish feasts and festivals, but it sounds more passionate than that to me. Jesus said it would be after the Tribulation. Maybe after the beginning of the Tribulation? Where else does the Word of God talk about the sun being darkened and the appearance of the Son of man? In Revelation, during the Tribulation. I would love to be able to write with great surety that Jesus is coming for us before the start of the Tribulation, but I think we better fasten our seatbelts. The ride might get bumpy.

Jesus continues in verses 32, 33 and 34, "Now learn the parable of the fig tree; when his branch is yet tender, and putteth forth leaves, ye know that summer is nigh: so likewise ye, when ye shall see all these things, know that it is near, even at the doors. Verily I say unto you, this generation shall not pass, till all these things be fulfilled."The fig tree Jesus is speaking of here is the nation of Israel. After years of wandering, the state of Israel finally once again became a nation at the conclusion of World War Two. Their first official day as a new nation was May 14, 1948. How long is a generation? Life expectancy in Israel in 2022 was 83 years. Jesus said, this generation shall not pass, till all these things be fulfilled. So, if you consider a child born in Israel when it became a nation in 1948, and add life expectancy of 83 years, you have the year 2031. It's getting close!

Don't misunderstand me, I'm not putting a timetable on when Jesus will return, however, I am running some numbers so you can understand how close we really are. There are Jewish people today who were born when Israel became a nation (the budding) who will not die before the Tribulation and Christ's return. Jesus said so Himself. Let's get ready!

There are three thoughts concerning the return of Christ, or the "Rapture" as some refer to it: Pre-Tribulation Rapture, Mid-Tribulation Rapture, and Post-Tribulation Rapture. The following are the basic beliefs of each...

The belief of a Pre-Tribulation return of Christ. Those who hold the Pre-Tribulation belief feel the rapture of the church is found in Revelation 4:1,2. They also believe Revelation 3:10 is a statement of Jesus that He will keep His saints from the hour of temptation (Tribulation). They believe the hour of trials or temptation is the time period of Revelation from chapter 6 through chapter 19, which covers much of the time of the Tribulation. They also believe I Thessalonians 1:10 and 5:9 to include the entire seven-year time of Tribulation.

The belief of a Mid-Tribulation return of Christ. With the Tribulation believed to be a period of seven years, this belief is that Christ will return for His Saints in the middle, or before the "Great" Tribulation part begins when the wrath of God is poured out upon the earth. This is also at times referred to as the pre-wrath position. Those who hold the pre-wrath position interpret Revelation 11:15 as meaning the church will meet Christ in the air, and then judgment will come upon the earth. It is believed, I Thessalonians 1:10 and 5:9, do not include the first 3 ½ years of Tribulation, but only the last 3 ½ years known as the Great Tribulation, due to the wrath of God being poured out upon the earth. See Revelation 20:4 and Revelation 13:5-8 (chapter 13 the Saints are present).

The belief of a Post-Tribulation return of Christ. This belief holds that Matthew 24:29-31 is clearly stating the Rapture occurs after the Tribulation, and that II Thessalonians 2:1-4 states the Antichrist will be revealed before the Rapture. In addition, Revelation 20:4-6 mentions the Saints who are killed during the mark of the beast, which occurs during the Tribulation. In Revelation 13:7, the Antichrist makes war against the saints, who are apparently still upon earth during this time of Tribulation.

Christ will deliver His saints from wrath by either rapturing them to Heaven, or guarding them during the time of wrath.

I cannot tell you, nor can anyone else, when Christ will return for His church; however, I must admit, while doing research for the original Bible study I taught at my church in Tennessee, and while studying to write this book, I did come across some Scriptures that leaped off the pages at me like never before. They have always been there, but I've come to see them in a new light.

For example, how does one reconcile what Jesus said in Matthew chapter 24, if you believe He is returning for His church before the beginning of the Tribulation? How does one explain the fact that according to John in Revelation chapter 13, the saints are still present, when this chapter is obviously during the time of Tribulation?

Directly after the close of the seven-year period of Tribulation, the battle of Armageddon is fought by Christ and his Saints. Then Christ sets up a 1,000-year reign of peace. I believe it is quite reasonable to believe Christ returns for His church just as the Tribulation is ended, and before the battle of Armageddon. This explains how the Saints are with Him at the battle. The devil is bound after this for 1,000 years. This is the Sabbath for our time.

> Revelation 20:1-4 KJV. "And I saw an angel come down from heaven, having the key of the bottomless pit and a great chain in his hand. And he laid hold on the dragon, that old serpent, which is the Devil, and Satan, and bound him a thousand years, and cast him into the bottomless pit, and shut him up, and set a seal upon him, that he should deceive the nations no more, till the thousand years should be fulfilled: and after that he must be loosed a little season. And I saw thrones, and they sat upon them, and judgment was given unto them, and I saw the souls of them that were beheaded for the witness of Jesus, and for the Word of God, and which had not worshipped the beast, neither his image, neither had received his mark upon their foreheads, or in their hands; and they lived and reigned with Christ a thousand years."

I would be happy to be incorrect in my calculations concerning the Tribulation and the return of Christ for His church. Regardless, I believe the best thing we can do for ourselves is just be ready: baptized in the Name of Jesus Christ for the remission of our sins and be filled with the Holy Ghost, as in the book of Acts.

Chapter 7
What Jesus Taught

It is extremely important that we teach, preach, and live what Jesus taught. There is certainly no room for error. If you were planning a very important trip, and someone familiar with the highways and roads gave you detailed directions, it would be important to follow the directions to the letter. One poorly thought-out short cut, or missed turn, and you would more than likely get lost, and quite possibly, not arrive at your desired destination at all.

David, King of Israel, stated, "Your Word have I hidden in my heart that I might not sin against You." There are people in our society who are living a life in sin and do not even realize it because of their lack of knowledge of Scripture. We are living in a time today where people consider themselves Christians (Christ-like) while at the same time are living in fornication, adultery, and other situations that the Bible clearly declares as sin. We must read and study the Scripture to know what it says so we are not deceived.

It has been said, you can live for Jesus however you may like, but if you intend to make Heaven your home, you must live for Jesus His way. In other words, there's only one way to Heaven, and it requires we do exactly as Christ has taught.

> John 3:1-3 KJV. "There was a man of the Pharisees, named Nicodemus, a ruler of the Jews: The same came to Jesus by night, and said unto him, Rabbi, we know that thou art

> a teacher come from God: for no man can do these miracles that thou doest, except God be with him. Jesus answered and said unto him, Verily, verily, I say unto thee, Except a man be born again, he cannot see the kingdom of God."

"Except." It sounds very matter of fact.

> John 3:6 KJV. "That which is born of flesh is flesh; and that which is born of the Spirit is spirit."

Nicodemus had no clue what Jesus was talking about. Nicodemus was stuck on natural terms. He was thinking of fleshly life. Jesus was speaking spiritual. The Kingdom of God is a spiritual realm. To get there, we must think and live in Spirit terms.

> In John 7:38 Jesus said, "He that believeth on me, as the scripture hath said, out of his belly shall flow rivers of living water." This is the whole key to eternal life. Pursuing Jesus as he taught that we must.

You may read the Bible from Genesis through Revelation and nowhere will you find the instruction to shake a preacher's hand, repeat a sinner's prayer, or join a church roll. This is earthy thinking, natural thinking as Nicodemus did. We must think Spiritual. What makes "rivers of living water" flow from a man? What was Jesus even talking about? He was again speaking in the Spiritual. The "rivers of living water" is the Holy Ghost that He told his apostles to receive once they traveled back to Jerusalem.

In John 14:16-18 Jesus said, "And I will pray the Father, and he shall give you another Comforter, that he may abide with you forever; Even the Spirit of truth; whom the world cannot receive, because it seeth him not, neither knoweth him: but ye know him; for he dwelleth with you, and shall be in you".

Jesus was speaking of this Comforter which was to come. This Comforter was the Spirit of truth. Jesus made it clear to His apostles, you know Him! He's with you! Here I am! But later that Spirit of truth shall be IN YOU!

> Acts 2:1-4 KJV. "And when the day of Pentecost was fully come, they were all with one accord in one place. And suddenly there came a sound from heaven as of a rushing mighty wind, and it filled all the house where they were sitting. And there appeared unto them cloven tongues like as of fire, and it sat upon each of them. And they were all filled with the Holy Ghost, and began to speak with other tongues, as the Spirit gave them utterance."

Jesus did say to them previously, "it shall be in you." What the apostles and others experienced in the upper room was exactly what Jesus had referenced in John chapter 14. When that Comforter comes, He will come inside you. He will dwell within you. And when He comes inside of you, you will speak in other tongues.

When God created man in the beginning, Genesis chapter two tells us God formed man from the dust of the ground. God has a man, but he was just a body. A body with no life within him. The Word tells us that God breathed His breath into man, and man did not only become a living creature, but he also became a living soul. Man was given a soul by the eternal breath of God. This is why humanity cannot be made joyous or happy by alcohol, drugs, or wealth and riches. Man has somewhere deep within an eternal soul that God put there with His own breath, and nothing can satisfy man except that Spirit of God that belongs there.

We have a multitude of churches that teach a multitude of differing doctrines. "Why do we have all these varying churches with so many doctrines and beliefs on how to get to Heaven?" you may ask. We'll cover that question in a later chapter, but suffice it to say, if we are not preaching, teaching, and living in accordance with the teachings of Christ, we are like the traveler who took an ill-fated short-cut or missed a very important turn.

Frankly, I'm not even interested in being a member of a church where no one is ever healed, delivered, or filled with the Holy Ghost. I'm not talking about "Accepting the Lord as your personal Savior." I'm talking about a life changing, Holy Ghost experience that elicits a response of praise and excitement. Jesus said, I have water, that if you drink, you'll never thirst again.

In Matthew 28:19 Jesus said, "Go ye therefore, and teach all nations, baptizing them in the Name of the Father, and of the Son, and of the Holy Ghost."

Let's take a close look at exactly what Jesus is saying here. He did not say, when you baptize people, this is what I want you to say. He said, baptize them in the Name of the Father, and of the Son, and of the Holy Ghost. So, what Name is He talking about? He said the Name. Obviously, Father is not a name. It is a title of someone who has a child. Son is not a name. That is simply a male who has parents. How about Holy Ghost, or Holy Spirit? This isn't a name either. It is the description of the Comforter, which by the way, Jesus said would come in HIS Name.

Jesus said, "I am come in my Father's name" (John 5:43) and in John chapter 17 while in prayer he stated, "I have manifested thy name unto the men which thou gavest me out of the world." My last name is Chesser because that was my father's name. My entire life I have carried that name. No matter where I traveled, I came in my father's name, Chesser. That name of Jesus is above every name. As a matter of fact, there's only one thing in all of creation that is held and esteemed higher than the Name of Jesus... and that is the Word.

> Psalm 138:2 KJV. "I will worship toward thy holy temple and praise thy name for thy lovingkindness and for thy truth, for thou hast magnified thy Word above all thy name."
>
> Luke 24:46-47 KJV. "And said unto them, thus it is written, and thus it behooved Christ to suffer, and to rise from the dead the third day; And that repentance and remission of sins should be preached in his Name among all nations, beginning at Jerusalem."

Whenever I baptize someone, I do not say, in the Name of the Father and of the Son and of the Holy Ghost, because that is not what Jesus said to do. I speak, in the Name of Jesus, or in the Name of the Lord Jesus Christ, for the remission of sins. Jesus expected His apostles, and everyone who follows Him, to know what that Name is.

The apostles did not misunderstand what Jesus was teaching them. As a matter of fact, Luke wrote in his gospel, that Jesus "opened their understanding, that they might understand the scriptures." Jesus would not have spent forty-two months teaching and preaching to these men, only for them to get it wrong after He ascended into Heaven. He opened their understanding so things were clear, and they would teach and preach exactly what people need to do to gain the Kingdom of God.

Not all the Scriptures are full of shouting and joy. There are some hard things in the Word of God. It's difficult for a pastor to stand in the pulpit and preach sin and call it by name. We all would love to have that feel good message where everything is sunshine, rainbows, and puppy dogs, but that's not always the case. Sometimes there are valleys, battles, and much spiritual warfare. Sometimes we have to take it by force.

> Romans 8:11 KJV. "But if the Spirit of him that raised up Jesus from the dead dwell in you, he that raised up Christ from the dead shall also quicken your mortal bodies by his Spirit that dwelleth in you."

What if that Spirit doesn't dwell in us?

Many years ago, when I was a young minister, I assisted an old time Pentecostal pastor in Missouri by the name of Cecil Smith. He used to say, "I've taken airplane rides, but one day I'm going to take a plain air ride."

We listen for a trumpet!

> Mark 16:17 KJV. "And these signs shall follow them that believe; In my name shall they cast out devils; they shall speak with new tongues; They shall take up serpents; and if they drink any deadly thing, it shall not hurt them, they shall lay hands on the sick, and they shall recover."

When we receive the Holy Ghost the way Jesus taught and the way the 120 did in Acts 2, on the day of Pentecost, we will receive power and authority. These are the signs which should follow us. There should be an anticipation and expectation of the miraculous.

Many churches across our society today are powerless, with no Spiritual authority whatsoever. Churches should look like the churches of the book of Acts. In Acts, they were experiencing instantaneous healings, miracles, people being delivered, and receiving the Holy Ghost with the evidence of speaking in other tongues. I contend, all churches should have this power. Jesus declared these signs should follow us. If we do not have these signs and miracles in our ministries and churches, we should examine our relationship with the One who grants such power and authority... Jesus!

Chapter 8
What the Apostles Taught

Peter and the other apostles followed Jesus for forty-two months. They saw Him open blind eyes, cause the lame to walk, heal lepers, raise the dead, and many other marvelous works. They heard His teaching concerning everything from prayer, fasting, and giving, to warnings of the end-time. Finally, before ascending into Heaven, He opened their understanding and sent them to Jerusalem to be filled with the power and authority of the Holy Ghost. By the time the day of Pentecost had come, and they received the Holy Ghost, Apostle Peter and the others were ready to answer the question, "Men and brethren, what shall we do?"

It was the day of Pentecost, the day of the Feast of First Fruits. It was commanded that the men of Israel travel to Jerusalem to celebrate this feast, give sacrifice, and give thanks. The Temple and streets were filled with thousands of Hebrew men who had gathered. In an upper room of the Temple were approximately one hundred twenty followers of Jesus who were doing what He had asked... return to Jerusalem until you are endowed with power from on high. While they sat together in this room, in one accord, or one desire and purpose, the Holy Ghost fell upon them. One of the notable signs that occurred was that all of them began to speak with other tongues... a language they had not learned in school... a language completely foreign to each of them. They spoke as the Spirit gave them the utterance to speak.

They spoke in various languages that all the Jews who were gathered for the Feast understood. Some from Mesopotamia, Judaea, Cappadocia, parts of Egypt, and other areas. They heard these simple Jews from Galilee speaking in tongues that they themselves did not even understand. The easiest assumption was that they were drunk, but Peter explained that was not the case.

Apostle Peter preached the first apostolic, Holy Ghost filled message as he attempted to explain to all these men what had just transpired. He quoted the Prophet Joel (Acts 2: 16-21), he quoted David, King of Israel (Acts 2: 25-28), and he even insulted them by informing the crowd that they were the ones who crucified the Lord Jesus.

> Acts 2:37-39 KJV. "Now when they heard this, they were pricked in their heart, and said unto Peter and to the rest of the apostles, men and brethren, what shall we do? Then Peter said unto them, Repent, and be baptized every one of you in the name of Jesus Christ for the remission of sins, and ye shall receive the gift of the Holy Ghost. For the promise is unto you, and to your children, and to all that are afar off, even as many as the Lord our God shall call."

The preaching of Peter pricked their hearts. It hurt them. They heard once again the words of the Prophet Joel, they realized David was writing about the Messiah, and they could not deny a great phenomenon had just occurred before their very eyes. Men and brethren, they asked, what shall we do (to be saved)?

Let's take another look at Peter's response and break it

down into pieces that are easy to digest. Peter laid it out step by step, as mentioned in an earlier chapter. It's worthy of another examination.

- Repent. A turning away. To turn aside from sin and the direction in which you are traveling. To change.
- And be baptized. This is an action of obedience. You have turned from your sin. In essence, you have died upon the altar. Time to be buried. Baptism is that burial.
- Every one of you. We all need baptism after we repent of our sins.
- In the name of Jesus Christ. This is the formula. The words to be spoken over you in baptism. Notice Peter did not say, in the name of the Father and of the Son and of the Holy Ghost. Peter knew exactly what Jesus meant when he spoke the words of Matthew 28:19 and Peter knew what that Name was that could wash away sins.
- For the remission of sins. It is an act of obedience and an act of faith. When we are baptized after repenting, baptism washes our sins away. When we come up out of that water, we have a clean slate.
- And ye shall receive the gift of the Holy Ghost. The Lord Jesus Christ has given us a promise. When we repent of our sins and are baptized in his Name, he will indeed fill us with the Holy Ghost. Our part is to continue to seek him and live for him.

There are times when a person comes humbly to the Lord, and He fills that person with the Holy Ghost before he/she is baptized. This was the case of Cornelius and his household, which we'll discuss in a bit. Others receive the Holy Ghost after baptism. The key is to continue to seek after Him and follow Him, and it will happen. It's a promise. He stands at the door and knocks. The Lord welcomes our hunger and rewards it.

> Acts 3:6-7 KJV. "Then Peter said, Silver and gold have I none; but such as I have give I thee: In the Name of Jesus Christ of Nazareth rise up and walk. And he took him by the right hand and lifted him up: and immediately his feet and ankle bones received strength."

Notice in the healing of the lame man Peter once again invoked the Name of Jesus Christ. There is no other Name that can bring salvation and healing.

> Acts 8:12-16 KJV. "But when they believed Philip preaching the things concerning the kingdom of God, and the name of Jesus Christ, they were baptized, both men and women. Then Simon himself believed also: and when he was baptized, he continued with Philip, and wondered, beholding the miracles and signs which were done. Now when the apostles which were at Jerusalem heard that Samaria had received the word of God, they sent unto them Peter and John: who, when they were come down, prayed for them, that they might receive the Holy Ghost: (For as yet he was fallen upon none of them, only they were baptized in the name of the Lord Jesus)."

The Apostle Philip traveled to Samaria to preach the Word of the Lord that he had received. In verse 16 Luke tells us that no one as yet had received the Holy Ghost there, but Philip had baptized them “in the Name of the Lord Jesus.” This is the exact way Peter told the crowd in chapter two they needed to be baptized. Philip was in agreement with Peter because he too understood the words of Jesus in Matthew 28:19. Philip also understood the Name is Jesus. After Peter and John laid hands upon those who had been baptized, they also received the Holy Ghost.

Acts chapter 10 tells the story of a devout man, named Cornelius. He was a leader of the Italian band—a group of soldiers—and a Gentile. An angel of God came to Cornelius and instructed him to send for Apostle Peter who was in Joppa, staying with a friend. Upon Peter’s arrival to Cornelius’ house four days later, Peter questioned why he had been summoned, but he realized due to the vision he had had on the rooftop (which is recorded earlier in chapter ten). God is no respecter of persons. With that in mind, this Jew entered into the home of the Gentile, Cornelius, to hear what he had to say. After Cornelius explained the visitation of the angel and how God had instructed him to send for Peter, Peter began to tell Cornelius and his household about Jesus, His ministry and His teachings.

> Acts 10:44-46 KJV. “While Peter yet spake these words, the Holy Ghost fell on all them which heard the word. And they of the circumcision which believed were astonished, as many as came with Peter, because that on the Gentiles also was poured out the gift of the Holy Ghost. For they heard them speak with tongues and magnify God.”

This chapter tells of the first time the Holy Ghost fell upon Gentiles. The Jews, which were with Apostle Peter, were astonished that the Gentiles received the Holy Ghost. They weren't even sure at that time whether the Holy Ghost was promised to the Gentiles. Now the question, how did they know that the Holy Ghost had fallen on Cornelius and his household? Verse 46 gives us the answer. "For they heard them speak with tongues." In chapter 11 when Peter is defending himself for going to the Gentiles, he explains to his counterparts in verse 15, "as I began to speak; the Holy Ghost fell on them, as on us at the beginning." The beginning Peter was referring to was the day of Pentecost, Acts chapter 2.

So, after Peter, and his six Jewish friends who traveled with him, witnessed these Gentiles receive the Holy Ghost, it stood to reason they now needed to be baptized.

> Acts 10:47,48 KJV. (Peter speaking) "Can any man forbid water, that these should not be baptized, which have received the Holy Ghost as well as we? And he commanded them to be baptized in the name of the Lord."

It wasn't a suggestion or just a thought that Peter had. Now that he had seen that God also intends for this precious gift to be given to Gentiles, as well as the Jews, Peter commanded they be baptized. And he specified that they were to be baptized in the Name of the Lord, just as he had preached on the day of Pentecost.

At a later time, Apostle Paul was traveling through the upper coasts and came to Ephesus. There he found certain disciples, twelve men to be exact. He asked the question, have you received the Holy Ghost since you believed? He came upon these men, who were obviously godly, Christ-like men, so Paul had an expectation that they were filled with the Holy

Ghost just as he and the other apostles were. These men responded that they had not even heard whether there be a Holy Ghost. Sensing something didn't add up, Paul asked, "How were you baptized?" They replied, "Under John's baptism," meaning John the Baptist. Paul explained to them that John indeed baptized unto repentance, but John taught that they should believe upon the One coming after him, that is, on Christ Jesus.

> Acts 19:5 KJV, "When they heard this they were baptized in the name of the Lord Jesus. And when Paul had laid his hands upon them, the Holy Ghost came on them; and they spake with tongues and prophesied."

When they heard there was more for them, they were hungry for it and accepted it. I've known good people who loved the Lord and lived for him according to what they knew or how they had been taught. They truly wanted to be saved but didn't know the entire truth of the Word of God. Sometimes we must be willing to dig deeper, or even change what we think we know, to realize and accept the full Gospel of Jesus Christ.

Once a friend of mine asked if I thought she was lost. She was a wonderful lady who attended what I'll refer to as a denominational church. They had a form of godliness but didn't experience the power of the Holy Ghost. She had visited my church several times and witnessed the demonstration of the Holy Ghost and was moved by it. I told her first of all, determining whether she was saved or lost was above my pay grade. Only the Lord knows our heart. I told her I know she's a wonderful lady and I believe she loves the Lord and truly has a desire to live for Him and be saved. I added that I believe she lives for the Lord the best she knows according to what she has been taught. But I asked her this question. If you see that there's more, if you see the power of the Holy Ghost and that He wants to fill you with his Spirit, wouldn't you want it? Of course, her answer was yes, I want the Holy Ghost.

There's many who attend church every Sunday and teach their children the Bible and how to be wonderful citizens, but they have not received the full truth. Many churches today have a form of godliness, but they do not teach all the Words of Christ. There's more for folks like this. We, as pastors and teachers, must teach all the Gospel of Jesus Christ: especially the power of the Holy Ghost, which is that Spirit that will one day raise us out of our graves.

> Colossians 3:17 KJV. "And whatsoever ye do in word or deed, do all in the name of the Lord Jesus, giving thanks to God and the Father by him."

Buy the truth and sell it not!

Chapter 9
Truth and Deception

A quick review of the previous chapter shows Matthew 28:19, Luke 24:45-49, Acts 2:37-39, Acts 3:5-8, Acts 8:15-17, Acts 10:44-48, Acts 19:1-7 and Colossians 3:17 endorse the Name for prayer, faith, baptism, and everything else we do either in our word or actions. That name being the Name of Jesus Christ.

The Bible, and historical facts, show the origin of the church (which teaches in the Name of Jesus and baptizes in the Name of Jesus) to be the Book of Acts, chapter two. This church is often referred to as the Apostolic Pentecostal Church. Apostolic because it follows the teaching the apostles brought forth in the book of Acts, and Pentecostal because the Holy Ghost was first poured out on the 120 in the upper room on the day of Pentecost.

This church, born on the day of Pentecost, which was filled with the Holy Ghost with the outward sign of speaking in tongues, is the Bride of Christ. It is not an organization any man constructed. One is born into this church just as Jesus taught Nicodemus in John chapter 3. One cannot achieve salvation by shaking a pastor's hand, joining a church roll, or reciting a sinner's prayer.

The beginning of the Roman Catholic Church is sometime during the first century, much later than the day of Pentecost and the live events written about in the book of Acts. The Roman Catholic Church had it's beginning, not in Jerusalem, or Israel, but in Rome. You may search the entire Bible but you will not find the birth or beginning of the Roman Catholic Church. It came to be, outside the realm of the Word of God.

What caused the Roman Catholic Church to be created? Remember this was during a time just after the resurrection and ascension of Jesus Christ. He instructed His disciples to return to Jerusalem until they were endowed with power, which was the infilling of the Holy Ghost in Acts chapter 2. What was birthed on that day was a ministry full of power and healing. Peter preached the first Apostolic, Holy Ghost filled message and three thousand were baptized in Jesus Name. Soon after, a lame man was healed at one of the gates of the temple by the commandment of Peter, in Jesus Name.

The miraculous was spreading across Jerusalem as this church grew. Thousands more were being baptized, receiving the Holy Ghost, speaking in tongues, and being delivered from sin. This not only caught the attention of skeptics, like Saul of Tarsus, but also the Roman government. Rome, at the time, was the world power, and they did not feel kindly to these Jesus Name preachers who were turning the world upside down.

Rome set out to stop this doctrine of Jesus from spreading, but the more persecution they brought, the more it spread. Now this Gospel was being preached, not only in Jerusalem, but it began to spread to other cities and towns as the Holy Ghost filled people of God fled Jerusalem for safety, taking the Gospel message with them.

So, Rome devised a plan...

If someone is sharing some truth (or good news) and it keeps spreading, but you have a desire to stop people from believing, what do you do? You realize you can't kill it or make it disappear, the more you persecute it the more it spreads, so you make a cheap copy. It's kind of the truth. It's enough truth that it sounds reasonable, but there's enough distortion and lies in it, that it's not the truth, therefore, ultimately it will not help people. This is what Rome decided to do. They created their own church and called it the Roman Catholic Church.

If you were going to start your own church in the first and second century, how would you do it? There weren't many other churches to copy or to gain ideas. As a matter of fact, at that time there was only one church. The church of the Book of Acts. Those folks who baptize in Jesus' Name and receive the Holy Ghost, speaking in tongues. There were other belief systems from other countries and peoples, but these were pagan. There was only one church. How do we design an acceptable copy?

Since this Apostolic Church came from the Jewish people, I believe the government of Rome studied the writings of the Jewish Old Testament. They probably figured that would give them a hint. Have you ever wondered why Catholic priests wear robes? Have you ever wondered why their leaders are called priests? Have you ever noticed the colors of the Catholic Church are red and purple? Have you ever noticed Catholic churches are arrayed in fine beauty, with many times gold cups, et cetera? Now, have you ever read the Old Testament? Sound familiar? Sometime toward the end of the first century and beginning of the second century, Rome officially founded the Roman Catholic Church and the deception was on.

Let's look at the teachings of the Word of God and compare them to the teachings of the Roman Catholic Church.

The Gospel of Jesus Christ, the Doctrine of Oneness, or One God: This is the belief that there is only One God, no separate persons of a Godhead. Oneness Doctrine teaches the entire Godhead dwells in Jesus Christ.

> Deuteronomy 6:4 KJV. "Hear O Israel: the Lord our God is one Lord."

> Isaiah 44:6-8 & 45:5 KJV. (Jehovah God speaking), "I am the first, and the last, and beside me there is no God..."

> Revelation 1:11. KJV (Jesus speaking), "I am Alpha and Omega, the first and the last..."

In Isaiah, God is telling us exactly Who He is, and we see in Revelation chapter one, Jesus is telling John exactly Who He is. Both are claiming to be the first and last. Jehovah even goes so far as to proclaim that there's no God beside Him. This is true and possible because there is only one God and thanks to the New Testament, we know his Name to be Jesus.

> Revelation 4:2 KJV. "And immediately I was in the spirit: and behold, a throne was set in heaven, and one sat on that throne."

This is the account as experienced by John. He saw the throne room of God. He saw one throne, not three, and he saw one sitting on that throne. Throughout the book of Revelation, he refers to that one as the Lamb, Who we know to be Jesus, the Lamb slain from the foundation of the world.

> Mark 12:29 KJV. "And Jesus answered him, The first of all the commandments is, Hear, O Israel; the Lord our God is one Lord."

Straight out of the mouth of Jesus himself.

> I Timothy 3:16 KJV. "And without controversy great is the mystery of godliness: God was manifest in the flesh, justified in the Spirit, seen of angels, preached unto the Gentiles, believed on in the world, and received up into glory."

God was... manifest in the flesh... His Name is Jesus!

> I John 5:7 KJV. "For there are three that bear record in heaven, the Father, the Word, and the Holy Ghost: and these three are one."

Don't be confused by what John said here. He did not say there are three persons in Heaven. He said "there are three that bear record." We all wear different hats in our lives. I am a pastor to my church folks. To my banker, I'm a customer or investor. To my grandchildren, I am Papa. I am many things to many people. My role changes often as I go about my day, but rest assured, there's just one of me. I can hear a sigh of relief from some of my friends and relatives.

- He is our Father in creation.
- He is the Son who brought redemption on Calvary.
- He is the Holy Spirit, who fills us with power.
- He is One.

> Colossians 2:9 KJV. "For in him dwelleth all the fulness of the Godhead bodily."

> Isaiah 9:6 KJV "For unto us a child is born, unto us a son is given, and the government shall be upon his shoulder: and his name shall

> be called Wonderful, Counsellor, The mighty God, The everlasting Father, The Prince of Peace."

The only way this is even possible... He is One. Let's take a look at a couple more Scriptures before moving on to the doctrine of the Trinity.

> Matthew 1:20 KJV. "But while he (Joseph) thought on these things, behold the angel of the Lord appeared unto him in a dream, saying, Joseph, thou son of David, fear not to take unto thee Mary thy wife, for that which is conceived in her is of the Holy Ghost."

> Luke 1:35 KJV. "And the angel of the Lord said unto her (Mary) the Holy Ghost shall come upon thee, and the power of the Highest shall overshadow thee: therefore also that holy thing which shall be born of thee shall be called the Son of God."

If you are a believer of the doctrine of the Trinity, did you see something very strange in what the angel Gabriel said to Joseph and Mary? He said to Joseph, Mary is conceived of the Holy Ghost, and he told Mary "the Holy Ghost shall come upon thee." So, if the doctrine of the Trinity is true, the Father isn't the Father at all. The Holy Ghost overshadowed Mary, making him the Father. How do we rectify this? "Hear O Israel, the Lord our God is One."

The Doctrine of the Trinity: The belief that there are three persons within the Godhead, Father, Son, and Holy Spirit, and these three persons have equal status and are equally divine.

The doctrine of the Trinity did not originate from the Bible. The council of Nicaea of the Roman Catholic Church, 325 AD (officially) established the doctrine of the "Holy Trinity". (See www.history.com.Counsel-of-Nicaea) The doctrine of the Holy Trinity is not taught in the Old Testament. In the New Testament the oldest evidence is in the Pauline epistles, especially II Corinthians 13:14 and I Corinthians 12:4-6. (The New Catholic Encyclopedia, Volume XIV, Page 306)

The term "Trinity" was originated by Tertullian, a Roman Catholic Church Father, who later became a priest. (New International Encyclopedia, Volume 22, Page 477)

In the third century, Tertullian explicitly defined the Trinity as Father, Son, and Holy Spirit and defended his theology against "Praxeas," though he noted that the majority of the believers in his day found issue with his doctrine. (en. wikipedia.org/wiki/Trinity)

The religions that Rome had the most problems with were the monotheistic – Judaism and Christianity. Because these religions believed there was just one God, they prohibited worshiping other gods. (www.crf-usa.org)

Baptism

Every person in the book of Acts and after were baptized in the Name of Jesus for the remission of sins. Before the Book of Acts people were baptized unto repentance according to John the Baptist's baptism. See Acts chapter 19. There is not a single example in the Bible of anyone being baptized with the formula, Father, Son, and Holy Ghost.

- The baptismal formula was changed from the name of Jesus Christ to the words Father, Son, and Holy Spirit by the Catholic Church in the second century. (Britanica Encyclopedia 11th Edition, Vol 3, ppg 365-366).

- The early church always baptized in the name of the Lord Jesus until development of the Trinity Doctrine in the second century. (Canney Encyclopedia of Religion).
- The baptismal formula was changed from the name of Jesus Christ to the words Father, Son, and Holy Spirit by the Catholic Church in the second century. (Catholic Encyclopedia, Vol. 2, pg 263).
- Christian baptism was administered using the words "in the name of Jesus" (Hastings Encyclopedia of Religion, Vol 2, pg 377).
- The use of a Trinitarian formula of any sort was not suggested in the early church history. (Hastings Encyclopedia of Religion, Vol 2, pg 378)
- Baptism was always in the name of the Lord Jesus until the time of Justin Martyr when Triune Formula was used. (Hastings Encyclopedia of Religion, Vol 2, pg 389).
- At first, baptism was administered in the name of Jesus, but gradually in the name of the Triune God, Father, Son, and Holy Ghost. (A History of Christian Thought by Otto Heick, 1965)

Sprinkling in Baptism

Baptism was changed from immersion to sprinkling by the Catholic Church in 1311 AD (My Catholic Faith).

For convenience and deception!

The Great Deception. That's what the Catholic Church was founded upon. We can't destroy the church of the Book of Acts, so we'll create a cheap copy, with a form of Godliness, but no power. We'll insert enough Jesus to make people feel accomplished, but it won't be the true Gospel of Jesus Christ, so none of it will matter.

Many souls are lost today because their pastors preach false doctrine, or they fear the faces, so they do not call out sin and preach the true gospel of Christ. The souls of those people will surely be lost, because of their own iniquity, but God will require the blood of those folks upon the hands of the preachers who failed, or refused, to preach truth.

Have you ever wondered why there are so many different churches preaching so many different doctrines? There's an explanation... here it is. For centuries there were only two churches which preached two doctrines: the Catholic Church, and the Jesus Name Holy Ghost filled church which was born in the Book of Acts. There were no Baptists, Methodists, Presbyterians, or the like. These churches had not even been thought of or considered yet. It all began to change in 1517. That's when Martin Luther, a Catholic priest, tacked his 95 Theses to the door of the Catholic Church in Castle Rock, Wittenberg, Germany. Luther condemned the excesses and corruption of the Roman Catholic Church, especially the Papal practice of asking payment, called indulgences, for the forgiveness of sins. This sparked the Reformation.

The Reformation was a major movement within Western Christianity in the 16th century Europe that posed a religious and political challenge to the Catholic Church and Papal authority. It became the basis for the founding of Protestantism, particularly the Baptist churches, Presbyterian, Calvinism, Lutheranism, and Methodism, from 1517 until

1648 when the Catholic Church signed treaties allowing coexistence with reformation churches which had formed.

While the Reformation served as a catalyst to bring people, hungry for God, out of the false teachings of the Catholic Church, those who founded churches and organizations failed to return to the full truth of the Oneness of God and baptism in the Name of Jesus, as in the book of Acts.

> Galatians 1:8 KJV. "But though we, or an angel from heaven, preach any other gospel unto you than that which we have preached unto you, let him be accursed."

Chapter 10
Martin Luther and His 95 Theses

Martin Luther was born on November 10th, 1483, in Eisleben, Saxony, Germany, and became a Roman Catholic Priest before his 25th birthday. He continued his studies, earning his Doctorate Degree in 1512. In addition to his priesthood, Luther was a monk, teacher, professor, and lecturer.

In 1516, Archbishop Albrect von Brandenburg appealed to Pope Leo X to allow indulgences, which was the charge of money to individuals to obtain full or partial forgiveness of sin, and allegedly shorten one's time in purgatory. Albrecht was deeply in debt, and Pope Leo X needed funds to build a new Saint Peter's Basilica in Rome. The two struck a secret deal, agreeing to split the money which was generated by the selling of indulgences.

Dominican Friar, Johann Tetzel, who was an agent of Pope Leo X, was sent to the Wittenberg, Germany region in 1517 to speak, and by doing so, raise funds through indulgences. Some members of the Wittenberg Church attended Tetzel's meetings and later showed Luther the letters of pardon they received through indulgences. Outraged at what Luther saw as a theological travesty, he began to pen his 95 Theses.

Apparently, Luther had no intention of parting ways with the Catholic Church, but rather his desire was a dialog to be opened concerning these 95 questions, or challenges, that he wished to be considered and debated, including the practice of indulgences. He sought to discuss policies of the Catholic Church which he found to be unbiblical.

Luther began to understand there were teachings of the Catholic Church that he could not find in the Bible.

- Where was the church's teaching concerning purgatory to be found?
- If one is saved by faith, why all the rules of penance and the payment to find forgiveness, through indulgences?

Luther further contended that Christ was needed in order for sins to be forgiven, not external requirements. Another of Luther's many concerns was that the church was teaching people that they could find forgiveness, without true repentance or godly sorrow, by paying money to the church.

By the end of October 1517, Priest Martin Luther had constructed a list of 95 questions, or topics for debate, which he had written in Latin and then tacked to the door of Castle Rock Church, Wittenberg, Germany on the last day of the month.

The list of the 95 statements of the Theses is easily found on the internet, however, allow me to list a few which I find most interesting.

- Theses Number 21. Those indulgence preachers are in error who say that a man is absolved from every penalty and saved by papal indulgencies.
- Theses Number 28. It is certain that when money clinks in the money chest, greed and avarice can

be increased, but when the church intercedes, the result is in the hands of God alone.

- Theses Number 32. Those who believe that they can be certain of their salvation because they have indulgence letters will be eternally damned, together with their teachers.
- Theses Number 36. Any truly repentant Christian has a right to full remission of penalty and guilt, even without indulgence letters.
- Theses Number 45. Christians are to be taught that he who sees a needy man and passes him by, yet gives his money for indulgences, does not buy papal indulgences, but God's wrath.
- Theses Number 48. Christians are to be taught that the pope, in granting indulgences, needs and thus desires their devout prayer more than their money.
- Theses Number 52. It is vain to trust in salvation by indulgence letters, even though the indulgence commissary, or even the pope, were to offer his soul as security.
- Theses Number 54. Injury is done to the Word of God when, in the same sermon, an equal or larger amount of time is devoted to indulgences than to the Word.
- Theses Number 66. The treasures of indulgences are nets with which one now fishes for the wealth of men.
- Theses Number 76. We say on the contrary that papal indulgences cannot remove the very least of venial sins as far as guilt is concerned.
- Theses Number 79. To say that the cross emblazoned with the papal coat of arms, and set up by the indulgence preachers, is equal in worth to the cross of Christ is blasphemy.

- Theses Number 86. Why does not the pope, whose wealth is today greater than the wealth of the richest Crassus, build this one basilica of St. Peter with his own money rather than with the money of poor believers?

Martin Luther's Theses was soon translated into German, English, and French and sent abroad and was viewed as challenging to the authority of the Catholic Church in Germany and Rome. Archbishop Albert of Mainz, disturbed by Luther's writings, sent copies to Rome in December 1517 requesting Luther be restrained.

Luther was commanded to recant his Theses a number of times, and after several refusals, the Pope issued an ultimatum threatening him with excommunication. On December 10, 1520, Luther publicly burned the Pope's letter. Priest Martin Luther was officially excommunicated by the Roman Catholic Church in January 1521.

On April 18, 1521, Martin Luther delivered a speech which included the following statement. "Unless I am convinced by the testimony of the Scriptures or by clear reason (for I do not trust either in the pope or in councils alone, since it is well known that they often erred and contradicted themselves), I am bound by the Scriptures I have quoted, and my conscience is captive to the Word of God. I cannot and will not retract anything, since it is neither safe nor right to go against conscience."

Luther's desire for questioning and debate, which was interpreted as defiance, is considered to be the beginning of the Reformation. It was a positive step to question Papal authority and false teaching, however, what came forth over the next century still fell short.

As I stated in an earlier chapter, while many preachers stepped forward, and many churches and organizations were founded, everyone fell short of returning to the original Gospel of Jesus Christ, which the apostles preached and taught in the Book of Acts following the day of Pentecost.

Chapter 11
Daniel

Before we enter into Revelation, the Great Tribulation, and who exactly is this Great Whore that John writes about, let's take a look into the Book of Daniel, since his prophecies set a foundation for end-time events. One thing we need to understand about the Book of Daniel, and the Book of Revelation for that matter, neither book is written in chronological order. Concerning the prophecies written in the Book of Daniel, some we find fulfilled during Daniel's lifetime, some during the time of Christ, and some we find will be fulfilled during the time of Tribulation. As we read the Book of Revelation, we see Daniel's end-time prophecies coming off the pages in fulfillment.

Daniel Chapter 2: Nebuchadnezzar's Dream

In the second year of the reign of Nebuchadnezzar, king of Babylon, the king had a dream. Unfortunately for the king, and the Chaldeans, the king could not remember the dream and threatened to cut the Chaldeans into pieces if they were unable to not only interpret the dream but remind him what the dream was. Of course, being a fair king and overall nice guy, the king offered rewards if they could fulfill his request.

After some wrangling and discussion, the Chaldeans said this was an impossible task. No king ever asked for so much because it's impossible unless the gods would help them. So, the king decided to do what seemed reasonable in his mind. He was going to have all the Chaldeans, magicians, astrologers, and wise men in all of Babylon put to death. This included Daniel, Hananiah, Mishael, and Azariah. When Daniel heard of this plan he appealed to Arioch, the captain of the king's guard, and then to the king himself.

Daniel 2:16 KJV. "Then Daniel went in and desired of the king that he would give him time, and that he would shew the king the interpretation."

The secret, as verse 19 calls it, was revealed to Daniel in a night vision, and Daniel blessed the Lord and went to Arioch to tell him he was ready to see the king to give him the interpretation.

The Dream

> Daniel 2:31-35 KJV. "Thou, O king, sawest and behold a great image. This great image, whose brightness was excellent, stood before thee; and the form thereof was terrible. This image's head was of fine gold, his breast and his arms of silver, his belly and his thighs of brass, and his legs of iron, his feet part of iron and part of clay. Thou sawest till that a stone was cut out without hands, which smote the image upon his feet that were of iron and clay and break them to pieces. Then was the iron, the clay, the brass, the silver, and the gold broken to pieces together, and became like the chaff of the summer threshing floors; and the wind carried them away, that no place was found for them: and the stone that smote the image became a great mountain and filled the whole earth."

The Interpretation

Daniel 2:37-44 KJV. "Thou, O king art a king of kings: for the God of heaven hath given thee a kingdom, power, and strength, and glory. And wheresoever the children of men dwell, the beasts of the field and the fowls of the heaven hath he given into thine hand, and hath made thee ruler over them all. Thou art this head of gold. And after thee shall arise another kingdom inferior to thee, and another third kingdom of brass, which shall bear rule over all the earth. And the fourth kingdom shall be strong as iron: forasmuch as iron breaketh in pieces and subdueth all things: and as iron that breaketh all these, shall it break in pieces and bruise. And whereas thou sawest the feet and toes, part of potter's clay, and part of iron, the kingdom shall be divided; but there shall be in it of the strength of the iron, forasmuch as thou sawest the iron mixed with miry clay. And as the toes of the feet were part of iron, and part of clay, so the kingdom shall be partly strong, and partly broken. And whereas thou sawest iron mixed with miry clay, they shall mingle themselves with the seed of men: but they shall not cleave one to another, even as iron is not mixed with clay. And in the days of these kings shall the God of heaven set up a kingdom, which shall never be destroyed, and the kingdom shall not be left to other people, but it shall break in pieces and consume all these kingdoms, and it shall stand forever."

These are the kingdoms of the beast in Nebuchadnezzar's Dream. Notice the material becomes less precious as the kingdoms become weaker.

Head of Fine Gold

Babylonian Empire (626 BC-539 BC) was a state in ancient Mesopotamia. The ruins of the city of Babylon are located in present day Iraq. Kings during Daniel's time were Nebuchadnezzar and Belshazzar.

Breast and Arms of Silver

Medes and Persians (539 BC—334 BC) Daniel dies during the kingdom of the Medes and Persians, approximately 538 BC. Kings during Daniel's time were Cyrus II (Cyrus the Great) and Darius I.

Belly and Thighs of Brass

Macedonian (Greek) Empire (334 BC-146 BC) King Phillip II of Macedonia is killed and Alexander the Great becomes king. Alexander the Great defeats the Persians and Egypt. He constructs a new city in Egypt named Alexandria. He would later conquer India. Alexander the Great dies in 323 BC.

Legs of Iron

Roman Empire (146 BC) Ancient Rome defeats Ancient Greece and becomes the new world power. They retain power until after the Day of Pentecost and the Book of Acts. Titus, a Roman military leader who later would become Roman Emperor, destroys Jerusalem in 70 AD.

Feet and Toes of Iron & Clay

End-time earthly kingdom with its alliances.

Stone

Jesus the Christ, Savior of the world. Kingdom without end.

Daniel Chapter 7: Daniel's Vision

Nebuchadnezzar has died, the children of Israel are still in Babylonian captivity, and now Belshazzar is king of Babylon. Daniel's vision comes during the first year of king Belshazzar's reign, which would be approximately 553 BC, fourteen years after the events of chapter six.

> Daniel 7:1-3—The great sea Daniel refers to is the Mediterranean Sea.
>
> Verses 4-8—The four beasts are the same four kingdoms mentioned earlier: Babylon, Medo-Persia, Greece, and Rome. (See Daniel 8:8, 11: 3-20). Compare verse 7 to Revelation 13:1,2. The little horn is the antichrist who speaks "great things and blasphemies" against God. (See Revelation 13:5,6).
>
> Verses 9-10—The Ancient of Days refers to God.
>
> Verse 11—The final destination of the beast will be the lake of fire. (Revelation 19:20, 20:10)
>
> Verse 12—The nations will be placed under the kingdom of Christ for one thousand years. (Daniel 2:44,45)

Verse 13—Coming in the clouds. (Revelation 22: 3,4)

Verse 21—See Revelation 13:7-10

Verse 25—Wear out the Saints of the Most High. Tribulation?

Verse 27—Christ and His saints will receive the promised kingdom. The everlasting kingdom.

We see much of Daniel chapter 7 played out throughout the Book of Revelation. I've always found it interesting to think that most of the prophecies proclaimed by the Old Testament prophets of God were mysteries to the prophets themselves. Daniel's vision would be no different. His vision disturbed him greatly. Finishing his vision, or prophecy that would become chapter 7, Daniel made it clear this was the end of the matter (verse 28) and that his cogitations, or carefully considered reflection not only troubled him but changed his countenance as well. But being a faithful servant of God, he kept the matter in his heart.

Chapter 12
The Great Whore ofRevelation

Revelation 17: 3-6 KJV. "So he carried me away in the spirit into the wilderness: and I saw a woman sit upon a scarlet coloured beast, full of names of blasphemy, having seven heads and ten horns. And the woman was arrayed in purple and scarlet colour, and decked with gold and precious stones and pearls, having a golden cup in her hand full of abomination and filthiness of her fornication: And upon her forehead was a name written, MYSTERY, BABYLON THE GREAT, THE MOTHER OF HARLOTS AND ABOMINATIONS OF THE EARTH. And I saw the woman drunken with the blood of the saints, and with the blood of the martyrs of Jesus: and when I saw her, I wondered with great admiration."

In Revelation Chapter 17, we read the description of this Mother of Harlots, which the Word of God also refers to as the Great Whore. This chapter in the Bible tells of the judgment brought to this Mother of Harlots. In verse six, another translation for the word "admiration" might be astonishment. Apostle John was astonished or amazed. What he was seeing had an emotional impact on him.

Picture the shock John must have felt at that moment. The woman was dressed in purple and red clothing, and adorned with gold, precious jewels and pearls, and she also had a gold cup in her hand. John sees inside this gold cup which was, no doubt, a beautiful piece, but inside he sees the cup is full of abomination, filthiness, and her very fornication, which in this instance is idolatry. He looks at the woman's face and she has a name written across her forehead for all to see: MYSTERY, BABYLON THE GREAT, THE MOTHER OF HARLOTS AND ABOMINATIONS OF THE EARTH.

Upon close examination, John realizes the woman is drunken, but not on wine or strong drink. He sees she is drunken with the blood of the saints of God and the martyrs who died for Jesus. John was emotionally impacted and astonished at the sight of all this.

> Revelation 17:9. KJV. "And here is the mind which hath wisdom. The seven heads are seven mountains, on which the woman sitteth."

If you do a web search and type in, "what city sits on seven hills," you'll find the answer to be Rome. What John was seeing was the Roman Catholic Church (The Mother of Harlots) sitting upon the beast, which is Satan himself. What other church is there that arrays herself in colors of purple and red, and adorns herself in gold, jewels, and pearls? Remember, the Catholic Church was founded upon deception. The entire purpose was to deceive the nations. This is listed as one of the reasons God's judgments fall upon her. See Revelation 18:23 and 20:8.

The ten horns John saw, according to verses 12 and 13, are ten kings which have received no kingdom yet, but will receive power as kings one hour with the beast. They will have one mind and shall give their power and strength over to the beast. They'll fight against the Lamb and be destroyed.

> Revelation 17:14 KJV. "These shall make war with the Lamb, and the Lamb shall overcome them: for he is Lord of lords, and King of kings: and they that are with him are called, and chosen, and faithful."

Drunken with the Blood of the Saints.

In 70 AD the empire of Rome, led by the military leader Titus, who would himself later become emperor of Rome, utterly destroyed the city of Jerusalem, just as Jesus had foretold in Matthew. Two years later Rome would begin the building of the Colosseum in Rome, which still stands to this day. It would take nine years to complete under the guidance of Titus and become one of the most amazing structures of mankind, given the time frame in which it was built. It would be inside the walls of this Colosseum that the woman sitting upon the beast would become drunken with the blood of the saints.

For the next several years the Coliseum would be a place of sport at the expense of innocent people. Keep in mind at this time in history there were no Baptists, Methodists, Presbyterians, or any other formed religious organizations. There were two churches at this time. The Roman Catholic Church and the church of believers directly out of the Book of Acts: Holy Ghost filled, tongue talking, Jesus' Name baptizing Saints of God. These other religious churches and organizations would not be formed until after Martin Luther's 95 Theses in Germany in 1517. There were certainly other "gods" and beliefs but only two who preached forth the Name of Jesus Christ. So, when you read about the "Christians" who were tortured, put to death, fed to lions, and torn apart by the teeth of other animals, you're not reading about denominational churches or organizations. You're reading about people who stepped right out of the Book of Acts. Perhaps some may have been those who were won to Christ in Rome by Apostle Paul himself.

The purpose was to kill off the Church, or do as much destruction and harm as possible, and by doing so, cause many to have a second thought about joining such a group and giving themselves to Christ in the Apostle's Doctrine. History tells us more than 3,000 Christians were killed, murdered if you will, within the confines of the Roman Colosseum. The Great Whore certainly was drunken on the blood of the Saints. Also slaughtered in the Colosseum were slaves, prisoners, and even some gladiators who were compelled to fight for the sport of the crowd or face death.

The Colosseum is not a positive structure. I have had friends in the past travel to Rome and post pictures of the Colosseum on social media, admiring its history and beauty. The Colosseum, in my humble opinion, is a place of abomination to God. It is nothing to see or visit. I have no desire to visit it or have my picture taken with it in the background. Within its walls God's true people died miserable deaths and the Lamb will one day take vengeance upon Satan and the Great Whore for their deception, destruction, and the spilling of the blood of the Saints of the Most High God.

> Revelation 18:1-3 KJV. "And after these things I saw another angel come down from heaven, having great power, and the earth was lightened with his glory. And he cried mightily with a strong voice, saying, Babylon

> the great is fallen, is fallen, and is become the habitation of devils, and the hold of every foul spirit, and a cage of every unclean and hateful bird. For all nations have drunk of the wine of the wrath of her fornication, and the kings of the earth have committed fornication with her, and the merchants of the earth are waxed rich through the abundance of her delicacies."

> Revelation 18:11-13 KJV. "And the merchants of the earth shall weep and mourn over her; for no man buyeth their merchandise any more. The merchandise of gold, and silver, and precious stones, and of pearls, and fine linen, and purple, and silk, and scarlet, and all thyme wood, and all manner vessels of ivory, and all manner vessels of most precious wood, and of brass and iron, and marble, and cinnamon, and odours, and ointments, and frankincense, and wine, and oil, and fine flour, and wheat, and beasts, and sheep, and horses, and chariots, and slaves, and souls of men."

The souls of men are just another commodity to this mother of harlots. They mean nothing to her. She does not care if you are free from sin, forgiven, saved, or even know Who the Lord Jesus Christ is. Her market is to build herself up at the expense of any nation, kindred, or man she may use for her own gain and benefit. The souls of men are merchandise to fill her house of gold.

The secrets that this abominable church has held tight for generations will be revealed on the last day Everyone will see her deception and she will be hated and reviled.

> Revelation 17:16 KJV. "And the ten horns which thou sawest upon the beast, these shall hate the whore, and shall make her desolate and naked, and shall eat her flesh, and burn her with fire."

Today, the Catholic Church is not only its own city, but it is a country, caring for its own funds in hidden accounts that even the city of Rome and nation of Italy cannot know or touch. When the wrath of the Lamb finally falls on the Great Whore it will fall fast and hard. Judgment will fall and there will be no hiding.

In the Catholic Encyclopedia you'll find the counter argument to this chapter. They will say the Catholic Church is not the Great Whore of the Book of Revelation. It's basically a "pay no attention to the man behind the curtain" argument.

> Revelation 6:9,11 KJV. "And when he had opened the fifth seal, I saw under the altar the souls of them that were slain for the word of God, and for the testimony which they held: And they cried with a loud voice, saying, How long, O Lord, holy and true, dost thou not judge and avenge our blood on them that dwell on the earth? And white robes were given unto every one of them; and it was said unto them, that they should rest yet for a little season, until their fellowservants also and their brethren, that should be killed as they were, should be fulfilled."

And then...

> Revelation 19:1,2 KJV. "And after these

things I heard a great voice of much people in heaven, saying, Alleluia: Salvation, and glory, and honour, and power. Unto the Lord our God: For true and righteous are his judgments: for he hath avenged the blood of his servants at her hand."

Chapter 13
Judgment

> John 12:46-48 KJV. (Jesus Speaking) "I am come a light into the world, that whosoever believeth on me should not abide in darkness. And if any man hear my words, and believe not, I judge him not: for I came not to judge the world, but to save the world. He that rejecteth me, and receiveth not my words, hath one that judgeth him: the word that I have spoken, the same shall judge him in the last day."

While Jesus was performing His earthly ministry, His goal was not to judge the world, or anyone. It was to save men from their sins. Many misinterpret this to mean Jesus doesn't judge us at all, and we can live by His grace, love and mercy, without concern about judgment. But it is extremely important that we understand what Jesus was saying in John chapter 12. Jesus made it very clear; he wasn't going to judge anyone during His ministry. That wasn't his purpose at the time.

But He then talked about the words that He speaks. His words were life and instruction. He was attempting to guide people on their journey. He informed the crowd that day, and you and me by His very words, that if we do not receive the Word, or instruction, that He teaches, there's One that will judge us on the last day. That One being the very words that came out of His mouth. The Word of God. Our Bible. We will be judged by the Word of God and whether we received it and obeyed.

When the local police pull you over for some infraction, they are not judging you. They are enforcing the law as they see it. If they write a speeding ticket, they will even say when they request you sign it that your signature is not an admission of guilt. Don't ask me how I know this, I just do. Later, depending upon whether you fight the ticket or not, you may stand before a judge. He is the one who will find you guilty or innocent. There is a place to be judged, and there are laws, rules, or words written that will be used to judge us. So, it is with the kingdom of God.

Those who stand before the judgment throne of God on that great day will find some books will be opened. One will be God's Word. We have the ability to read it for ourselves now. We won't be able to plead ignorance on that day. For those who wander through life wishing God would speak to them, He did. Pick up the book and read it. Study it. We will need to know exactly what it says to be saved.

Another book to be opened is apparently a book of our own life. Revelation chapter 20 tells us we will be judged according to those things which were written in the books, according to our works. What you have done in your life, the words you have spoken, good or bad, are being recorded and will be reviewed on the day you stand before God.

Thankfully we have repentance that, according to the Bible, causes God to choose to not remember our transgressions when He forgives. Those transgressions are wiped away. Then God will have the Book of Life opened. Jesus talked about this book during His earthly ministry. Luke tells us that Jesus sent out seventy of His disciples to preach the

Kingdom. When they returned, they were ecstatic that even the devils were subject to them through the Name of Jesus. Jesus encouraged them to not rejoice because devils are subject to them, but rather rejoice that your names are written in Heaven. It is of utmost importance that our names be written in the Book of Life. One will not inherit everlasting life unless our names are written therein.

As stated in a previous chapter, our names are written in the Book of Life when we repent of our sins, are baptized in the Name of Jesus Christ for the remission of sins, and receive the gift of the Holy Ghost. If we are filled with His Spirit there will be no reason for us to stand in front of God at the white throne of judgment, since we will have been raptured with the church and already stand with Christ.

As human beings, we have a tendency to compare ourselves with others. I suppose we do this so we don't feel so bad about ourselves. After all, at least we're not the worst sinner in the room, right? The problem with that kind of thinking is this. When we are judged, we are not going to be judged against each other. You may be hoping there's someone you know standing nearby when you stand before God that you know was a far worse person in life than you. Nice try, but that's not going to help, because God is not going to judge you against them, and vice versa. We will be compared to His Words and how we obeyed. David, King of Israel proclaimed, thy Word have I hid in my heart that I might not sin against you. It's all in the Word... life, breath, and even eventual judgment.

> Mark 9:43-48 KJV. "And if thy hand offend thee, cut it off: it is better for thee to enter into life mamed, than having two hands to go into hell, into the fire that never shall be

> quenched; where their worm dieth not, and the fire is not quenched. And if thy foot offend thee, cut it off; it is better for thee to enter halt into life, than having two feet to be cast into hell, into the fire that never shall be quenched; where their worm dieth not, and the fire is not quenched: And if thine eye offend thee, pluck it out: it is better for thee to enter into the kingdom of God with one eye, than having two eyes to be cast into hell fire; where their worm dieth not, and the fire is not quenched."

Jesus taught love and forgiveness but repeatedly warned about hell and judgment. We deceive ourselves if we convince ourselves that grace is going to ultimately cover all our wrongdoing after our lives are over. I have heard it referred to as "cheap" grace. It's a grace people cling to, but it doesn't help us in the end. It's really not worth anything. We cannot take advantage of grace and mercy by continuing in sin. Apostle Paul wrote to the church in Rome, "What shall we say then? Shall we continue in sin, that grace may abound? God forbid" (Romans 6:1-2a). Things will not end well for us if we try to take advantage of the mercies of God based on cheap grace.

Some ask, would a loving God really send people to hell? If you'd like to dissect it, God is not sending anyone to hell. He has taught in His Word the way to everlasting life. It is up to each of us to read, study, learn, and follow His plan. Where we spend eternity is really about the choices we make. I believe it would be safe to say the number one reason people are lost is due to disobedience.

> II Peter 3:9 KJV. "The Lord is not slack

> concerning his promise, as some men count slackness; but is longsuffering to usward, not willing that any should perish, but that all should come to repentance."

There will be no excuses on that day. We won't be able to claim ignorance. We won't be able to blame the pastor, the deacons, or our Sunday school teacher. Maybe it's true, we were mistreated along the way and experienced "church hurt." Hey, I'm a believer in "church hurt." I have suffered from "church hurt" myself. People aren't perfect and sometimes people do hurtful things that hurt others. But that will still not be an excuse. People who experience church hurt need to forgive, heal, and move along. Go to a different church if you need to. Position yourself away from the one or ones who hurt you. Leave them in God's hands. Our number one goal in life has got to be making sure our names are written in that Book of Life.

> Matthew 22:37-40 KJV. "Jesus said unto him, Thou shalt love the Lord thy God with all thy heart, and with all thy soul, and with all thy mind. This is the first and great commandment. And the second is like unto it, Thou shall love thy neighbor as thyself. On these two commandments hang all the law and the prophets."

I have spoken with people who have told me they came to the Lord because the minister preached hell is hot and you're going there if your heart is not right with God. While I can appreciate that kind of preaching, and I certainly do agree with the sentiment, I believe to live a successful life in Christ we're going to have to grow past the fear factor. Any style of preaching, or any Scripture that causes a stir in us to make a positive move toward Jesus, is a wonderful thing. We need more stirred hearts. But to live for the Lord through the ups and downs of life, we need more than just a fear of hell. The key lies within what Jesus said according to Mathew 22:37-40. If we can develop a true love for Jesus and His word as we grow in Him, we will make it to everlasting life. You see, we don't want to hurt the ones we truly love. We will do things that we never thought we would do, if it's for the ones we love. If we love the Lord the way Jesus describes how our love should be, we will love Him with our entire being, inside and out. That love will motivate us, drive us, and keep us moving forward.

Much of the way we live our lives is due to the things we give ourselves to. The music, the media, the books we read, the time we spend, or do not spend in prayer. All these things have an effect on our everyday existence. The world is a very noisy place. Maybe this is why Jesus said when you pray, go to your closet and shut the door. Maybe Jesus is trying to tell us to live for Him most effectively, we need to shut the world out.

> Revelation 20:10 KJV. "And the devil that deceived them was cast into the lake of fire and brimstone, where the beast and the false prophet are, and shall be tormented day and night for ever and ever."

I thought I would add this Scripture for those who are hoping for total annihilation, as opposed to everlasting torment. If we're choosing to not live for the Lord, it may be comforting to think that when we die, that's all there is to it, but that's not the way my Bible reads. We need to prepare.

In verse eleven, John sees a great white throne and Him who

sat upon the throne. John then saw the small and great being brought forth to stand before the Judge. That's when the books were opened as referenced earlier. Also, the sea gave up the dead in them, and death and hell delivered up the dead for judgment. Every man was judged according to their own works (verse 13).

> Revelation 20:15 KJV. "And whosoever was not found written in the book of life was cast into the lake of fire."

The Lord will take no pleasure in this. God manifested himself in flesh and died upon Calvary so men and women could avoid this. The stripes upon His back were strong enough for healing. The blood that drained from His body was good enough to provide our redemption. Those folks verse 15 are speaking about are people who either deliberately disobeyed the Word of God or were deceived.

We must make Everlasting Life our top priority, above anything else in life. Some people do not live for the Lord because it is inconvenient for them. Yet they go to work. They make their house payments, and car payments, go grocery shopping in busy markets, and do all sorts of life things that are inconvenient. Life itself is often simply inconvenient. Yet we do life every day.

I'll even confess to you right here in writing that yes, living for the Lord can at times be inconvenient. But I do it. I attempt to do it with all my heart. Because the payoff is Heaven and, while it may at times be inconvenient in the flesh, it will be worth every minute of inconvenience on the day I inherit my brand new mansion.

In the City where the Lamb is the Light!

Chapter 14
Heaven

> John 14:1-3 KJV. "Let not your heart be troubled: ye believe in God, believe also in me. In my Father's house are many mansions: If it were not so, I would have told you. I go to prepare a place for you. And if I go and prepare a place for you, I will come again, and receive you unto myself; that where I am, there ye may be also." Jesus

Jesus isn't inviting you to go to Heaven as a guest. He says, "I want you to go live with Me there. Come be with Me. There are mansions. There are streets made of pure gold. Come live with Me there, forever." There's a difference between an invitation to come be a guest, and an invitation to come live with Him. He didn't say the Father is building a guest house. He's building mansions. I've never lived in a mansion before. Actually, I don't even need one in Heaven. It would be enough just to live and reign with Christ forever. But if He's passing out mansions, why not claim one?

> I John 3: 1-2 KJV. "Behold what manner of love the Father hath bestowed upon us, that we should be called the sons of God: therefore the world knoweth us not, because it knew him not. Beloved, now are we the sons of God, and it doth not yet appear what we shall be: but we know that, when he shall appear, we shall be like him, for we shall see him as he is."

> I Corinthians 15:51-55 KJV. "Behold, I shew you a mystery; we shall not all sleep, but we shall all be changed, in a moment, in the twinkling of an eye, at the last trump: for the trumpet shall sound, and the dead shall be raised incorruptible, and we shall be changed. For this corruptible must put on incorruption, and this mortal must put on immortality. So when this corruptible shall have put on incorruption, and this mortal shall have put on immortality, then shall be brought to pass the saying that is written, Death is swallowed up in victory. O death, where is thy sting? O grave, where is thy victory?"

Think of time just as a quick moment, eastern skies, clouds splitting. Think about the change that will occur in your mortal flesh if you are filled with the Spirit of Christ. We will turn from mortal flesh to immortal spirit in a moment, in the twinkling of an eye.

> Romans 8:11 KJV. "But if the Spirit of him that raised up Jesus from the dead dwell in you, he that raised up Christ from the dead shall also quicken your mortal bodies by his Spirit that dwelleth in you."

Matthew tells us one day the disciples came to Jesus and asked who was the greatest in the kingdom. I could be overthinking this, but I can't help but picture the disciples flexing and posing and attempting to gain the attention of Jesus so He would name them. But what Jesus did say could not have been further from what they were probably expecting. He called a little child, who apparently had been playing nearby, and sat him in the middle of all the disciples.

Taking The Kingdom

"Except ye be converted" Jesus began, "and become as little children, ye shall not enter into the kingdom of heaven. Whosoever therefore shall humble himself as this little child, the same is greatest in the kingdom of heaven" (Matthew 18:3).

If we want to be the greatest in the Kingdom of Heaven, or even get to the Kingdom, we must be converted and become as little children. I will say this, if you want an honest answer about anything, ask a child. They won't hold back. Many times, they'll tell you what they're thinking without you even asking. Children are innocent. That is until adults start polluting their minds with prejudice and hatred.

Little children are the purest form of humanity so long as they are left to be children. Children are trusting. They'll believe what you say until you give them a reason not to. You can tell a child there's a monster in their closet and they'll believe you, and you can tell a child Jesus loves them, and they'll believe that, too. A child will never hate another child simply because they are of a different race or nationality. Those are behaviors taught them by adults. Children are eager to go, run, play, and learn. Have you ever looked deep into the eyes of a child and seen all that wonder and amazement that lives in there? Jesus said, if we want to inherit the Kingdom of God, we've got to be like that.

Why is that? Why must we intelligent, mature adults become like children? I would contend it's about trust. It's about honesty. It's about adventure. Have you ever looked deep into the eyes of a new convert who has just been filled with the baptism of the Holy Ghost? It's life changing for that person. Next time you're around someone who has just received the Holy Ghost look deep into their eyes. You'll see wonder, amazement, and adventure.

Sometimes the trusting part can be the most difficult. John trusted everything was going to be alright as Jesus looked down upon him, dying on the cross, and directed him to care for Mary, His mother. Peter trusted everything was going to be alright as he and John were thrown into prison for bringing healing to a lame man. Paul no doubt trusted everything was going to be alright as he regained consciousness after being stoned in Lystra and thrown out of the city, left for dead. After tending to his wounds and trying to get a good night's sleep, he and his companions continued their journey preaching the Gospel.

One way or another, everything's going to be alright. We must not live for what we can gain in this mortal life. We must look to Heaven. Our goals need to be long term. We all have some short-term goals we hope to achieve, but let's not forget to look long term. There's a reward far greater than that next new car, bigger house, or dream vacation. Let's not allow our eyes to get off the prize.

> Revelation 21:1-4 KJV. "And I saw a new heaven and a new earth: for the first heaven and the first earth were passed away, and there was no more sea. And I John saw the holy city, new Jerusalem, coming down from God out of heaven: prepared as a bride adorned for her husband. And I heard a great voice out of heaven saying, Behold, the tabernacle of God is with men, and he will dwell with them, and they shall be his people, and God himself shall be with them, and be their God. And God shall wipe away all tears from their eyes; and there shall be no more death, neither sorrow, nor crying, neither shall there be any more pain: for the former things are passed away."

John paints a beautiful picture of what Heaven, or the new Jerusalem as he calls it, will be. You see, John was a Jew, and the center of his universe had been Jerusalem. That had been the capital of the Hebrew people for generations. Jerusalem was a very important place, not only to John, but all the Jewish people. But John saw something new. He saw a place coming down from God that had been prepared for God's people, the Bride of Christ. John quickly adopted this new place and determined that's where he wanted to be. A place with no pain, no tears, no crying, no death, no sorrow, and God would be there to be our God. The NEW Jerusalem.

In Revelation 21:6, Jesus proclaimed: It is done. Judgment has come and it's time for the Bride to be united with the Lamb, in the new Jerusalem. This is it, John, I'm wrapping things up. Welcome home!

In Revelation Chapters 21 and 22, John describes this beautiful new city which he saw. Twelve gates constructed of twelve giant pearls, with the names of the twelve tribes of Israel, twelve foundations, named for the twelve apostles, walls of jasper, a city of pure gold, no need for a sun because the Lamb will be the light, a pure river of the water of life, a tree of life on either side of the river, no more curse, and we shall see the face of the Lamb.

> Revelation 22:17 KJV. "And the Spirit and the bride say, Come. And let him that heareth say, Come. And let him that is athirst come. And whosoever will, let him take the water of life freely."

"Amen. Even so, come, Lord Jesus" (John the Apostle)

Printed in the USA
CPSIA information can be obtained
at www.ICGtesting.com
LVHW061647200823
755758LV00048B/1063